Mad Blood

For now these
hot dayes, is the mad blood stirring.

—William Shakespeare
Romeo & Juliet, Act 3, Scene 1

Edited by

Jim Keller
&
Murray Moulding

Colorado

Copyright © 2021 Jim Keller & Murray Moulding

All rights reserved.
All rights return to the authors upon publication.
No part of this book may be used
or printed without permission
except in the case
of brief quotations
in critical articles or reviews.

For information contact:
Pearn and Associates, Inc.
victorpearn@ymail.com

First Edition

Cover by Megan Ryan

Library of Congress Control Number:
2021941890

ISBN 978-1-7357731-2-4 Paperback

Published in the United States of America

Rita Brady Liefer

1930 - 2021

"Once upon a time there was this woman."

Nesting Doll

ACKNOWLEDGEMENTS

Grateful acknowledgment is made to the following publications, and their editors in which these poems first appeared:

The Colorado Sun, "One-Sided Conversation With The Covid-19 Coronavirus (with apologies to Dr. Seuss)"

Finishing Line Press, "Down River," "Icicle Medicine."

The Human Touch, "Behind The Mask I've Worn So Long."

Santa Fe Literary Review, "Near Bear's Ears."

TABLE OF CONTENTS

Foreword
Murray Moulding & Jim Keller xv

POETRY

Pandemic Necessities
Joe Hutchison 1

River Parade Blessing
Bill Tremblay 3

Finding Snow On Good Friday
Kathryn Winograd 5

Our Marriage Under A Pandemic Moon
Kathryn Winograd 6

What Can I Say, What Can I Know
Jim Keller 7

Orioles
John Macker 8

Covid-19, What I Miss
Lorrie Wolfe 9

Covid-19 At The Entrance To Purgatory
Lorrie Wolfe 10

Small Things May Make For Good Poems
Lorrie Wolfe 12

A Grown-Up Letter To Santa Claus On Independence Day July 4, 2020
Lorrie Wolfe 13

Behind The Mask I've Worn So Long
Art Elser 15

A Ghazal Struggling To Breathe
Jean Bell 17

Epidemic
Murray Moulding 18

Reclamation
Page Lambert 19

About Myself
Linda Hogan 21

The Names Of Creeks
Linda Hogan 22

The Mountain Between
Linda Hogan 23

Eagle Feather Prayer
Linda Hogan 24

A History Of Kindness
Linda Hogan 25

When The Body
Linda Hogan 26

Fences
Linda Hogan 28

Tulsa
Linda Hogan..29

Isn't It Love
Linda Hogan..31

Desert Monsoon
Anita Jepson-Gilbert..32

Through A Broken Looking Glass
Anita Jepson-Gilbert..33

Our Baffling Bill Of Rights
Anita Jepson-Gilbert..34

An Invitation To Grief
Amy Wray Irish..35

Autobiography Of Sunlight
Gia Nold..36

Grandinroad
Gia Nold..37

Zoom Nation
Mike Coste..39

The Journey
Lynda La Rocca..40

One-Sided Conversation With The Covid-19 Coronavirus (with apologies to Dr. Seuss)
Lynda La Rocca..42

Zoom
Maria Berardi..43

Origin Story
Maria Berardi............... 44

Covid Kintsugi
Judyth Hill............... 45

Dice Cup
Sandra S. McRae............... 49

Advance Copy Of Eulogy
Sandra S. McRae............... 51

Mama!
Sandra S. McRae............... 52

The Sphinx's Riddle
Robert Cooperman............... 53

The Grass Cure
Robert Cooperman............... 54

DNA Testing
Robert Cooperman............... 55

Henry And The FBI
Robert Cooperman............... 56

Perpetual Care
Robert Cooperman............... 57

The Christmas Thief
Robert Cooperman............... 58

I Look At Poetry As An Affliction
Gerard Smaldone............... 59

Somehow The Soul Still Soars
Jared Smith............... 61

Ode To The Future In This Pandemic (A Pantoum)
Carol Guerrero-Murphy 62

Zooming With The Horse And 7 Variations
Carol Guerrero-Murphy 63

Remembering Laura Maze And Donna Jean As The Same Woman
Padma Thornlyre 65

China Cat
Padma Thornlyre 67

Above And Below In The 21st Century
Lisa Zimmerman 71

Another Full Year
Lisa Zimmerman 72

Time For Everything
Jon Kelly Yenser 73

Invitation Of The Moths
Jon Kelly Yenser 74

On RTE. 66
Jon Kelly Yenser 75

My Grandchild
Veronica Patterson 76

Meditation On This Autumn
Veronica Patterson 78

It Is The Swallows
Veronica Patterson 79

Passionate Pilgrim
Marcia Jones 80

Leave The Balcony Open
Marcia Jones 81

Yellow Sky
Marcia Jones 82

senior living
Peggy Knoepfle 83

Lynching
Lon Wartman 84

The Lilacs Are Gone
Kyle Laws 86

The Angle Of Things
Kyle Laws 87

A Break To Heal
Kyle Laws 88

Who Heard The Sunset Yowl?
Kyle Laws 89

Grappling With A Bit Of Astrophysics And The Optimum Wrinkle Cream
Frank Coons 90

Ursa Minor Or Whatever The Opposite Of Chevalier Is
Frank Coons 91

Numbers And Figures
Michael Henry 92

Andy Warhol's Silver Clouds
Michael Henry *94*

Poem Beginning With Lines From Bob Dylan
Michael Henry *95*

Near Bear's Ears
David Feela *96*

The Other One
David Feela *97*

Before Bed
David Feela *98*

Down River
Renee Podunovich *99*

Icicle Medicine
Renee Podunovich *101*

Four Elements
Kim O'Connor *103*

A Tarbert Evening (1968)
Kathleen Cain *105*

Lace
Kathleen Cain *107*

Dear Stranger
Kathleen Cain *108*

prayer against corona
Victor Pearn *109*

Dancing In The Streets
Victor Pearn *110*

Integrity
Victor Pearn 111

Who's In Heaven?
Victor Pearn 112

Sometimes
Linda Keller 113

Sacred Space
Linda Keller 114

Whatever It Was
Linda Keller 115

Headlines
Linda Keller 116

Contributors *117*

FOREWORD

In January 2003, First Lady Laura Bush invited Sam Hamill, editor of Copper Canyon Press, to a symposium celebrating the poetry of Walt Whitman, Langston Hughes, and Emily Dickinson. This was, of course, in the mad run-up to the Iraq War, and Hamill refused the invitation to the White House out of protest and a call to conscience. Instead, he asked several friends to compose protest poems, to have them delivered to the First Lady on the day of the soon-cancelled symposium, February 12, 2003. Word got around and poets across the country began writing and held open readings everywhere. Thus that day marked the beginning of the Poets Against the War movement taken up by writers all over the US. Despite their efforts, in March of 2003, the *Shock and Awe* campaign was launched by the Bush administration, and the first bombs were dropped on Baghdad, lighting up the night sky and embroiling the United States in a conflict that would smolder over the next eleven years.

"For now, these hot days, is the mad blood stirring," became the motto for a new literary and arts journal born in Evergreen, Colorado, in June of that same year. These words, spoken by Benvolio to Mercutio in *Romeo and Juliet*, seemed ideally suited for the conflict in 2003, as well as the turmoil under which our nation struggles today.

Padma Thornlyre edited and produced the journal *Mad Blood* for several issues and included in its pages poetry, prose, photography, and visual arts from writers from all over the West. Many of them performed in a Mad Blood reading series in Evergreen, likewise, promoted and hosted by Thornlyre, drawing more and more poets into the *Mad Blood* community. The readings ran until the pandemic shut down personal gatherings. Well before the pandemic, Padma turned over leadership of the project to Jim Keller and Murray Moulding, who hosted the readings, then replaced the monthly readings with a virtual journal that includes many familiar authors, as well as some new voices. The works featured in the journal from June 2020 to December 2020 have been published here. To include all the poems published since the beginning would have been daunting indeed; hence this edition appears with hopes for a fuller volume to come.

Murray Moulding & Jim Keller

Joe Hutchison

PANDEMIC NECESSITIES
for Melody

*I am speaking now of people made
desperate by the apprehensions
of their being shut up.*
                —Daniel Defoe

Lucky life isn't one long string of horrors . . . .
                —Gerald Stern

Told he's allowed just three
    4-paks of toilet paper, this
        wiry guy in front of me
with seven in his cart
bickers with the checker,
    locks horns, then rips
        into her. The girl pales
but keeps on reciting
    the store's policy on
        contagion. Those of us
in line—all masked,
some gloved in nitrile blue—
    watch the guy as if in slow
        in slow motion fling
a fat 4-pak at her head, see it
knock her glasses off. She
    staggers back, hands raised,
        splayed and shaking.
"Hey!" someone barks.
Another: "Back off, you
    asshole!" The man flips
        a pink, freckled
    middle finger at us
just as a khaki-clad guard
    bulls up behind him,
hammerlocks his arms. The guy
    twists, but the guard—a good

        head taller—drags him
    out into the parking lot.
Their red-faced scuffle
    plays out in a big window,
        and we all lean slightly
    toward it to catch
their muffled curses . . . .
    Suddenly the guy breaks
        free and bolts. The guard,
    winded, stands his ground,
panting into his shoulder mic.
    The man in flight digs
        into his jacket, fishes out
    a key fob and aims it. A gray
SUV's parking lights flash
    in answer, and the guy scrambles
        into the driver's seat.
    The engine *vrooms*,
and the car jerks and squeals
    away, rocking wildly
        into the misty
    April twilight. No one
speaks. Now the checker bends,
    snatches up her glasses,
        slips them on, and without
    a word waves me forward
to ring up my lucky life's
    pandemic necessities:
        dark red wine, a wedge
    of Parmigiano, a slab
of sea-salted dark
    chocolate, and two
        bunches of incandescent
    yellow daffodils
for the one who gives
    my heart its clearest reason
        to keep on beating.

Bill Tremblay

RIVER PARADE BLESSING

The river flows, I take notes. Colored flags
pass by. Gold sparkles of sun on water ripped

by rocks, gold bells of trumpets. I straggle
off the path and nearly step on two yellow-

bellied water snakes twisted together, their
onyx-bead eyes so keenly pleased at coupling.

The river fleshes its scales in ripples. The
only solitude as the river adds its white noise.

I get the petal-softness of its liquid silk.
Water molecules in the beaks of skimming

swallows. Ranks of tubas, the high school band
led by a majorette who strikes sparks from

steel taps on her tasseled white boots,
Knights of Columbus, the VFW, who will

never fit into the uniforms they marched in
after the landings at Anzio, Monte Casino

bombed from B-24s until Italian children
bounce on their bellies waiting for it to end.

Buicks gleaming with prom queens
waving in pink ball gowns year after year,

droplets of history are the work of the sun,
the twinkling eye of the Commonwealth,

chrome batons spun high into elm leaves
of Memorial Day, a river of *penitentes*, lungs

clogged with lives, Main Street flooded with
swollen tongues singing *We are coming, Father*

Abraham. Of the sun's fire a pile of ashes if
I don't kneel at the water's edge and douse

my brow. Ten thousand years of parades,
scores of Empires, people's lives, the camels

they ride. They burn in love-fires, have children,
die, move toward perfection of the species,

a race who know what the river knows,
blessings from all we don't understand.

Kathryn Winograd

FINDING SNOW ON GOOD FRIDAY

The sky, not even bruised,
spills its light, blue
as the petals of the wild iris
wound in their buried boats
beneath the morning fire
ash I throw to the cold
wind, again. I think
the iris, named for a rainbow
goddess of such purity
and loved so by a god,
must belong to early
summer, and so it will not
rise yellow-eyed and soon
in my dark harbors of grass
and aspen root no matter
what I dreamed last night
or whom I wept for
or how long I linger in this gold
slip of sun on the porch step.
Maybe tomorrow, in tiny
pockets of earth and worn
granite or in the last snow
that does not drift away,
I will find the pasque-flower.
And quiet and trembling for its
purpled flesh and early
blossom, I will call
it love. And sorrow, too.

OUR MARRIAGE UNDER A PANDEMIC MOON

"By this time we are both an open secret."
—James Wright

I dried the last pan, let it clatter into the shelf beneath the oven, still warm from our chicken and sweet potatoes. You had hurt yourself again, the tender threads of your knees torn I feared when you pulled your boot off untied. I didn't say anything, silence these days a companion of the house like the field mouse we can't find in the shed that shreds through the new bag of oiled sunflower seeds you drove up from the plains, their black and white husks like scattered boats. I pulled on my boots, lifted slightly the backdoor to unhook its crooked latch and walk into the cold evening, to see the pink moon, I told you. The wind wound itself around me, lifted my hair, touched my face. I placed my feet like loaves of bread in the snow thaw, a piping of hidden birds the whole time I walked. The moon was chalk, a stone statue, a face cratered, a doorway of light, everything I'd ever heard of, the old grass beneath it the color of wild mustard, and the new grass, where the neighbor's plow had shredded the snow for us all winter, mute, dark-winged. I wondered why it mattered, thirteen full moons this year, moons named *Wolf* or *Snow* or *Worm* before we even settled indoors this moment to live separate from everyone else we knew. The angus cows were nowhere, feeding elsewhere on scraps of winter grass. I missed their breathing. I missed their heads swinging from their necks thick as obsidian, totems or sentries watching me pass. The wind knocked me down the lane, a slab of wind until I curved south: the moon my shoulder. I wanted this to be beautiful; I wanted this to be about love, even the bluebirds ploughing the air. I kept watching the moon, thinking it pink, thinking this will never be again, this new world awful and frightening, and you, quiet in the loft, waiting for me. Then, the moon lifted my shadow like a feather, and a bird I startled from the bunched grass carved itself into an arrow, the sky a wild creature.

Jim Keller

WHAT CAN I SAY, WHAT CAN I KNOW

of Black Lives Matter?
Ensconced in white privilege
my candle's feeble light
is lost beside the black
sun of racism
I have no skin
in this game
I have no standing
in this court
My knee grounded
a feeble token beside
one crushing a neck

John Macker

ORIOLES

I wrote about finishing off a fifth of
tequila last night so I wouldn't have to. A
pair of orioles make a soft landing in
the yard and harangue me from a mimosa
branch about the bitter states of America. They
summer up here, as bright and orange as the sun.
They winter in Mexico in an orange grove at a
cartel hacienda and entertain in between fiestas.
Their impatient *chut chut chut whew whew* says it all.
If I could fly, I wouldn't believe so much in
ghosts, their turbulence is nuanced. I know
an actress who moonlights as a flight attendant
until Hollywood calls.   The last time I flew
I brought the coffee heavily and unsteadily to
my lips, not so much as a wolf nap.
These trying days must border on the holy
everything about this country that's extreme
sprouts wings   in spite of everything, spring
hurls mantras of resurrected color at the earth.

Lorrie Wolfe

COVID-19, WHAT I MISS

I miss the first sight of stacks
of blueberries by the front door
of my grocery store, the glint of sun
hitting the plastic edges
of their delicate cases,
that color—unearthly blue
like deepest ocean on a June afternoon,
blue as a baby's new eyes that see all,
a dustier blue than the cups of columbines
on a hillside just below timberline,
peeking from under snow-kissed aspen trunks.

I miss a big hug from Kate,
whose wide hips and soft bosom
are the timeless embrace of Mother Earth,
wrapping and forgiving me for whatever
I may have done, or even considered doing;
whose generous smile says she really is glad
to see you and that things
will soon come right again.

Kate, whose daughter works at the last open café
downtown, where you can still get eggs
done just right, and where the coffee,
Oh God, the coffee is a rich, brown heaven, and where

who knows for how much longer
they can—or really should—hold on
trying to be   normal,
as if this fear and isolation were just
any last year's Tuesday at 2:00.

COVID-19 AT THE ENTRANCE TO PURGATORY

What you notice first is the silence
everywhere. And the dry leaves. No wind rustles them today.
The trees are Shakespeare's "bare ruined choirs,
where none or few do hang."

At first it seems there are no cars moving, then you realize
a few intrepids still rove the streets, each one holding
only a driver. No passengers. Isolation
in a metal carapace. A two-ton exoskeleton.
Are these travelers the essential workers?
Will they, can they provide food, nursing?
Will they be the ones to care for you or your loved ones?
Are *they* safe?

The street is empty in front of your house except for cars parked,
stopped dead in driveways and gutters before silent yards.
Eight of the twelve are pickup trucks.
You had not remembered there were so many.
The working hands of neighbors now somber and stilled.

You are glad to be here. You are outside,
walking to the mailbox, hoping
someone you know has written you a letter, proof
a friend remembers who you really are.
You bless the mail carrier who is not stopped
from her duty by rain nor gloom nor dark of pandemic.

The light that bathes the street is solemn, doleful,
as if the cloud-draped sun is suspended
above a soundless void,
waiting for children to spill from the mouths
of houses invisibly boarded against the virus
but not yet abandoned in a plague-proofed city,
a state, a country.

Notice your breath, waiting to find its safe place
inside a snow-globe's bubble,

until our nation raises its star-spangled head once again
and becomes a place proud to be from,
a home to belong to.
You are still   here.

SMALL THINGS MAY MAKE FOR GOOD POEMS

> "How shall the heart be reconciled to its feast of losses?"
> — Stanley Kunitz, *The Layers*

I couldn't get my mind around it
overwhelmed with the ten o'clock news and
your name in the paper,
that aching list of losses.

Tonight I thought of you
sharpening those yellow number two's
back when we were too young to follow the news
and coming to a point was easy.

Tomorrow, tomatoes will be rooting,
just starting their heroic scarlet journeys.
Heirlooms, Early Girls, and Better Boys,
futured viridian limbs penciling out along each wire cage

Tomorrow there will still be daisies out back
Their titanium-white petals
like young girls' lace collars
encircling bee-infested cadmium centers

Such temporary colors, too soon gone.
I tried to write about one small thing
but everything was too large today
and I grow farther from my roots every day.

A GROWN-UP LETTER TO SANTA CLAUS ON INDEPENDENCE DAY JULY 4, 2020

Soul of kindness,
we could use you now
in this summer heat.

In winter,
Be-furred in your cherry suit
and stovepipe boots,
your heart bursts with joy
at the children who crowd your throne
and scramble onto your lap.

Let us come to you now
in our grown-up clothes,
pocked with tears and grief,
marked by tear
gas and painted protests.

We roil in the streets,
horrified at the sycophants and maligners
who pose as leaders, all the while,
hiding behind their assumption of
guilt-before-inquiry

Instead of tea into a harbor,
today we spill salt water and blood
seeking restitution, not revolution

Santa, we have been *good* for so long,
waiting in patient belief
that our country's holiday
will bring exactly what we
have been hoping for
in our most treasured,
secret wishes —
not skates or bicycles, but
the promises of freedom

fulfilled as if by your timeless magic,
or at least, after all our hard work —
our goodness rewarded.

Art Elser

BEHIND THE MASK I'VE WORN SO LONG

I've broken out in hives, first time in my life,
eighty-four years without ever having them.
I'm sure it's from long-buried stress, born
in a war over fifty years ago. In those days,
I couldn't trust people on the street and open-air
market, as I drove an open jeep to the airfield.

*Does that man looking at me plan to lob
a grenade in my jeep? Does that scowling
woman walking next to the road have a gun
tucked in her long black sleeves?*

Today before I shop at the local grocery store,
I fit a mask to my face and pull on gloves
to protect me from a virus that's killing many.
I cannot trust the people I see in the store.
Any could carry, pass me the virus, casually.

*Did that woman, that one not wearing gloves,
handle this box of cereal I just put into my cart?
Did that unmasked man cough on my apples?
Did a stocker with the virus shelve my cheese
or carton of milk while not wearing a mask?*

My every-day fear in that long-ago war was
that this was the day when that golden bullet,
the one with my name inscribed on it in script,
would find me as I passed by, taking my life.

Today the death wouldn't be sudden, riding
a bright red tracer stream from a gun hidden
in a tree line or the edge of a jungle clearing.
Today it would come from a cough, a sneeze,
a covert viral bullet on something I touch,

then touch my face in an unconscious gesture,
to scratch an itch, wipe away laughter's tears.

And so, fears held tight many years in the
fist of memory are loose, crawl up my arms
in itchy red blotches.

Jean Bell

A GHAZAL STRUGGLING TO BREATHE

Grief dons a mask, but suffering
has already infected the lungs of the world
love and fear, equally, struggling to breathe.

Coal dust clings to him like an aura, smudges
his face, chisels a living from deep in the earth
Appalachian despair struggling to breathe.

Sirens scream into night, careen down
empty streets, around abandoned corners
moonlight survival struggling to breathe.

Too slow to awaken, she's undone by a dream
the bear closing in as she runs — lungs bursting —
panic and daylight struggling to breathe.

Tulips released from earthy internment
shout red and yellow to a rising sun
roots under dark ground struggling to breathe.

Trail into wilderness, uncharted terrain
no bridge across the Hallelujah River
hope for deliverance struggling to breathe.

Murray Moulding

EPIDEMIC

The night air breeds contagion. The fan in the window sways
lazily back and forth. Each time it passes this one spot, a whisper
comes in. I am in bed with the measles, or I think it was measles.
We are in Mercury retrograde. Last night we were on the beach
at 7:43 to watch a full moon break over the horizon. A glow
at the edge of the clouds, then the moon itself, in the clear.
"I believe in all things visible and invisible," say the Anglicans.
Yesterday, I walked past a woman kneeling in her yard,
     administering
CPR to a man on his back. "Come on, come on," she kept saying.
Then I heard the sirens. They tell us germs are everywhere,
     on the night air,
out of nowhere. Today, I shall bundle Kate and Shakira
     onto our small boat
and head north, up the Indian River, into sunlight and fresh air,
     beyond beyond.

Page Lambert

RECLAMATION

They say the traffic in London has killed the song of the nightingale. When they serenade each other, they sound more like the honking of horns, the squealing of brakes, and so the nests
                lie
                    empty.

Yet a coyote sought shelter in a Chicago Starbuck's last month, the closest thing to a cave he could find, stood shaking next to the cooler in the dark corner with the Odwalla juices and the caffeine drinks and the mineral water from Fiji. Just last weekend, in Santa Fe, in the hours before dawn, on the Plaza while the town slept, a mountain lion leapt through the door of a *jewelry* store, leaving a spider web of broken glass. In Denver, raccoons pilfer garbage beneath city streetlights.

Sleek Peregrines, with nesting boxes built into skyscrapers, stalk the pigeons cooing from the rooftops. Owls swoop down alleys, between buildings, hunt the falcons which hunt the doves. Moose leave the northern wetlands, trek long-legged across Wyoming's Red Desert, nip purple blossoms from our alfalfa field, half-way between here and the short grass prairie; black bears forage in suburban kitchens, paw their way to the shallow end of public pools.

Elk herds cross highways, leap burrow ditches, tear through *fences*, travel the old migratory routes to the land their ancestors once grazed, while in Billings the city council passes laws prohibiting dogs in public parks. Yet, they say that New York City, without man to trim its hedges, prune its trees, mow its grasses, replace roads and bridges and traffic signals, would soon be overrun with feral dogs, yellow-eyed cats, and ivy.

New York City, without man or woman to tame it, would within two hundred years begin to crumble, in half a century would turn to dust, turn back to the earth within a millennium. Wars would fade from the horizon, borders disintegrate, walls come tumbling down, pandemics pass from memory. Silt would rise in the dams, rivers return to their beds. A new human would rise, begin the task all over again, would carve flutes from the branches of cedar trees, piano keys from the tusks of mammoths, stain glass from the sands of the Sudan, sew drums from the skins of buffalo.

Songs would rise from its thirsty throat, deep and guttural. Eventually, the trilling of women would pierce the night sky, slice through the blue darkness like a sleek whale. Nightingales

>would return
> to their songs.

Linda Hogan

ABOUT MYSELF

My people come from this land once plenty.
out from caves to this world
of tall grasses
where earth rises and falls
as the ribs of a body,
bones, some in their hiding,
some the great mountains.
We found the waters
with their own breath and tides
following the moon.
Those first human signs are still here
in this two-legged animal,
imperfectly woven
but twined well enough
to be a burden basket
filled with the gatherings
of a day's work I carry home
on this bent back
with a common hunger.
Walking in the moonlight,
ribs like those bones of land,
my hands carrying a bag of greens,
wild turnip, onion, mushroom,
a single flower,
I, too, am merely one
brief living shine.

THE NAMES OF CREEKS

Old Woman Creek.
One Dog Creek.
Dead Horse Creek.
It makes a person wonder what happened there,

but Sand Creek we remember
and we'd like to go back
long before it happened
and turn time around
instead of people.

Before I was born
the plans for killing were made
down the hill from where I live
at Bear Creek.

Chivington was present
with other humans
with no compassion
 in their hearts
and they made plans against nations
they called Friends.

It haunts me now to know
from here came that ominous plan
of blood and fallen bodies
from dark hate and hunger,
desire for the land or gold
when the old ones knew
each plant, each stone,
each story of what was before them
in every place,
but not what happened next

*[Chivington: Main Planner of the Sand Creek Massacre]

THE MOUNTAIN BETWEEN

Down at Bear Creek
that runs through our town
like something is chasing,
that's where the Massacre
was planned.
From down there, up a mountain
and down to a valley
is the little cabin where I live.
Old mother closed her eyes
when I learned this story,
then said, Good thing there is a mountain
between you and their words.

EAGLE FEATHER PRAYER

I thank the eagle and Old Mother for this prayer
I send to earth and sky
and the sacred waters. I thank Old mother
and the golden eagle, the two who taught me to pray
without words. They instilled a part of me
no named by anatomy books.
They gave that part their own perfect names
And so I stand here now
facing you and the rest of creation.
I send this prayer of gratitude to those who risk their lives
for clean, sweet water,
and once again there is the great silence
of what happened to the buffalo enclosed in cutting wife
one night as if dark magic was at work.
And so hard it is to pray for the shooters
who laughed about hitting the girl with one good shot.

We love our horses. We love the dogs. They have helped us before.
We love the wildness of buffalo herds. To love is the labor of
       humans,
but I don't know what happened to the shooters,
their purpose for being, although with no words,
and with the part of my named self
I hold this fan from Old Mother and the eagle
and with all I have, send a prayer
so very silent.

                                             [Standing Rock Prayer]

A HISTORY OF KINDNESS

When a child becomes an animal in clouds
changing forms to other creatures,
our grief has become a kindness to the sky.

When the hay is baled and you worry, what if
a mouse or snake was inside,
that is a gentleness.

When the horses are fed and all that's left is a withered apple
for a woman to eat, and she is grateful
for the life of all things so she feeds it to the horse,
that is a good heart.

When you are gentle to the skin of others,
touching them softly, speaking with gentle words,
it is compassion.

When there is agreement among those
who might have argued instead,
it is a gift to all.

When skin is the first organ to form in the body of a woman,
and skin is the largest organ we have,
that is a mother's first protection.

If you still love the invisible place where a child once stood,
the heart recalling her soft hair, her long dark legs,
that is the spaciousness of memory.

And when you pick up the old woman on the worn road
to help her home and you see that inside
she has nothing, you give her the food you have.

You give the only can of coffee, then start her woodstove
and leave your coat behind on purpose.
What else would a real human do?

WHEN THE BODY

When the body wishes to speak, she will
reach into the night and pull back the rapture of this growing root
which has no faith in the other planets of the universe,
but her feet have walked in the same bones
of the ancestors over long trails,
leaving behind the oldest forest. They walk on the ghosts
of all that has gone before them, not just plant, but animal, human,
the bones of the ones who left their horses to drink with them at the
spring running through earth's mortal body
which has much to tell about what happened that day.

When the body wishes to speak from the hands, it tells
how it pulled children back from death and it remembers every
    detail,
washing the children's bodies, legs, bellies, the delicate lips of the
    girl,
the vulnerable testicles of the son,
that future of my people brought out of the river
in a spring freeze. That is only part of the story of hands
that touched our future.

This all started so simply, just a body with so much to say,
one with the hum of her own life in a quiet room,
one of the root growing, finding a way through stone,
one not remembering nights with men and guns,
the ragged clothing and broken bones of my body.

Let's go back to the hands, the thumb that makes us human,
but don't other creatures use tools and lift what they need,
intelligent all, like the crows here, one making a cast of earth clay
for the broken wing of the other, remaining
until it healed, then breaking the clay to fly away together.

I would do that, too,
since a human can make no claims
better than any other, especially without wings,
only hands that don't know these intelligent lessons.

Still, I think of the willows
made into a fence and even cut, they began to root and leaf,
then tore off the wires as they grew.

A human does throw off the bonds if she can, if she tries, if it's
        possible.
The body is so finely a miracle of its own, created of the elements
of anything that lived on earth
where everything that was
still is.

FENCES

I will never think of them in the same way
watching this woman with her brown skirt
throw her own body against the fence,
trying to climb.
Believing in freedom
she hits it like the wind
and still it keeps her
from the water of another life,
the dream of another imagined world
until finally she does nothing but, with all her might,
she throws a rock over it
so something reaches that destination.

What about the meek, the wretched,
the tired, the poor and yearning, the vulnerable
ones in their countries of life thieves
who, like the vigilantes,
have no fiber of mercy, no humanity
that has ever lived to be free,
no hunger or pain about them,
not for the fragile being of any child.
They forget they were the land thieves,
the takers, the soldier gangs.
Like their poor dogs
they will find some other bone
to crack, some gristle,
some other nerve of mercy
for the penned, fenced people
like birds with wings of beauty
locked in a small cage
in a room with windows
to the desired world.

TULSA

Not the white men riots of the past,
but only yesterday
a man was shot in the back by a police officer.
She was white, he black, she a medic
who didn't help him, nor did the others who arrived.
For minutes they watched while they could have
saved him but for his skin.
I try to imagine watching a man die
because they fear or hate the darkness
of a human, a man who had no weapon, not even words,
the man who began his day like any other,
saying to his wife, Helene, I'll be back early today.
I'm taking you out for Mother's Day.
She sat under the lamp with her tea,
finishing the hem of their daughter's jeans
before she left for work. The pictures on the table
of their children, children with more and less melanin
in their skin. They are beautiful and smart, loved,
and doesn't it scare a father that they are learning to drive?
Does it scare you that one dates a white boy and they might love?
What does the officer think
as she stands, watching the man lose blood and die?
That she might get in trouble? That she won't?

2.
I am a dark woman. Dark. Darker. Even Darker.
A Chickasaw woman from the very old days,
but if the police saw me today they would think me white,
maybe whiter than them. I can pass.
They would save me, not knowing
the history in my skin
that lies to them
and how I might be thinking of them with fear
or something worse.

3. Soccer
The kids from the tribe had a chance
to go to a soccer game, so they kept up their grades;
the game was their reward. Excited, they rode the bus, so quiet,
and sat on the bleachers, learning the game, watching,
until the white men above them poured beer
on the children's color of skin, poured beer on their coats
from the unknown reservation world
from which they came.
White Men.
Native Children.
I wonder, if like the policewoman,
their soul came from some other place.

ISN'T IT LOVE

Isn't it love that pulls me into the world,
the morning sky colored by rouge and becoming
deep and clear blue, as though a spring of water has entered
red earth. That is the place our relatives said the buffalo went
to wait for some safe day so their spirits could return.

Isn't it love that brings me to rise early to feed the horses their hay,
to clean the burro who sleeps in a pile of shavings
with the horse watching over her
in the manger, so young and surprised at the sounds she can make,
The horse is more silent. She is always the first
to receive, before the small burro she looks after.

But isn't it love that brings me to carrying grain, hay,
cleaning the water
when some days I would like to sit with the trees and a book
or paper and ink,
or look down to the field where deer and turkey
roam, where some trees are now down on their sides after the flood
came through and took away so much of the world.

When the old man told me it could happen, it was hard to believe
such a small creek might rise up and rage that way
but it became a river. Now I watch what will happen next spring
as this world is changed
and see what comes from that water.

Then, what can I call it at night when I open the wine
for a glass with my simple meal, so all alone without a heart
to beat against mine, or a hand to caress this body
so I think of that speaks so gently with myself,
then I caress the cat, brush the dog, take night hay to the horses
along with their sweet for the night.

Anita Jepson-Gilbert

DESERT MONSOON

By July
we grow weary
of the desert—
her barrenness,
her parched arroyos,
her cloudless, endless blue.
We wait, facing south, wistful
for those first welcome signs,
like bales of Mexican cotton,
to come tumbling over ragged mountains.

There, they gather and spin
then weave themselves
into the canyon, dyeing quickly
into long, black drapes
that sweep coolly
across our nakedness.
And when they lift,
we dance to songs of faithfulness,
 and even the land runs wild.

THROUGH A BROKEN LOOKING GLASS

We walk gingerly
through the country,
as through a field
of broken glass,
refracting memories
from the past,
shattered but still
reflecting softer visions
and words that heal
our deep divisions.

How does glass
so smooth with light
become sharp enough
to scratch and kill,
so dark it wants
to do us ill?

What power lies
beneath the glass
to make me smile or cry?
Could it be the silver
That's mixed with grains of copper
and painted on the other side?
Or is it the shattered face I see,
looking back at me?

OUR BAFFLING BILL OF RIGHTS

We, the People,
are frequently right
where we need to be,
but sometimes we're left
behind, without due rights.

Some claim they are right
when they're dead wrong or
add pepper to the salt of truth
or change their mind, signaling
left but in an instant, turning right.

We, the People,
often say or write
what we think is right,
but then realize sometime
later that it was never really true.

We honor many rights--
human rights, animal rights,
rights to guns and religious rites.
Some think we have far too many,
while others claim we have too few.

Is their party on the right,
just around the corner, or is
it much too right for our taste?
It's so confusing now to know just
where a grand old party really stands.

We, the People,
cherish our sacred rights.
We talk and write about them
though we're just not sure which rights
are right for us, right now, in a righteous land.

Amy Wray Irish

AN INVITATION TO GRIEF

When I hold in the cold breath of my sorrow
so long that I numb from the inside out, then
I must draw a bath, raise water so hot that steam
billows up to erase me. In that blind, white-out
world I write an invitation on the mirror,
my finger streaking through the fog like tears.

The water scalds my skin awake
as I step in. Boils away my fear. Melts
my frozen pain and loss. In heavy sheets
my glacier shears, cracks and crashes down
into the churning ocean below. Then
all doors open to allow Grief in.

And how she howls through. A banshee
that shreds away security, control. But
I need the freedom of her keening cry, need
to release layer after layer of weight.
Her wailing ensures I will not succumb
to a frigid end of feeling and join the dead.

So I let her visitation slam me down,
a tsunami against my naked shores. With her
I am all storm, water pounding on water,
an infinite ocean pouring forth. On and on
until my tidal wave is spent, the icy darkness
washed from every deep and hidden part.

Then Grief recedes. Ebbing away the pain,
but leaving me a taste of ache. An absence
that is not empty. A low and constant throb
like a beating heart. A reminder to embrace
with warm arms all who have died. A reminder
that the heat of flowing tears means I'm alive.

Gia Nold

AUTOBIOGRAPH OF SUNLIGHT
After Nancy Pendleton's Reflecting Sunlight (mixed media)

Climbing a ladder

I'm the girl in clay

My costume is a square

I'm a machine making a cross

A red map in India Ink

Left   right   down   up

yellow is next

and the woman on her knees

who prays

Are you being a tongue again?

Arms are   dark

Mother that says   "Go"

I love the buzz when colors mix

My heart is a dot

I surround you with squares and metallic circles

GRANDINROAD

Shapes are everywhere

The older tree is a puppet

A black and white bird

sings   Will you marry me?

      I can see your world

You are a dot next to golden rocks

The cloud is a woman in   Peruvian hat

      an indigenous virgin

She is heavy with

      arms that are wings

      huggin' all

Trees all around her

People of all ages

Held hands

It's hard to see smiles

The lime-green sky

      blocks their faces

Twigs are letters

or messages of colors

      blue-green-yellow-orange

My eyes are

      twins

The blue moon does not stop blessing

I'm told there is Nothing in this portrait

People is in trouble   The world   ugly

      seeing the road up to it

The large blue space   is me

There are   Breathe   Breathe   signs everywhere

Mira   Mira

     right there in front of things

Mike Coste

ZOOM NATION

Yes, we're the Zoom Nation,
Awash in alienation,
Expressing our frustration
      At the voting booth.

Look into a box
At everyone who talks.
Don't wanna get the pox
      To tell the truth.

Our backgrounds are all fake.
We live on scotch and cake.
A virtual mistake
      This remote machine.

Not wearing any pants.
Just listen to the rants
Of all the sycophants
      In quarantine

I haven't cut my hair
And all I do is swear
As I refuse to share
      My computer screen.

Let's hope that this all ends
While I still have some friends
And Dr. Fauci sends
      An approved vaccine.

Lynda La Rocca

THE JOURNEY

When twilight falls upon the land
and everything is still,
and purple shades to indigo
on grass and tree and hill,
before the moon shines yellow in
the autumn of the year,
the silver dog so quietly
creeps nearer, nearer, near
the window of the cottage with
its door barred fast and tight,
and begs for sanctuary from
the terror of the night.

He whimpers, poor old fellow, and
he scratches at the wood.
Please let me in, he seems to say,
and know that I've been good
and faithful to you all my days;
I've never wanted more
than kindness and a quick caress.
Please—open up the door.

The latch is lifted suddenly
and from inside is heard
a mingling of voices, shouts
and laughter, and one word
the grizzled dog had longed to hear
for many a lonely day.
"Come!" Master cries, and in he bounds,
who'd been so long astray.
"We thought you lost forever, boy!"
 The family clusters 'round.
"We searched and called and sought, but you
were never to be found.
Yet now it seems a miracle

has brought you safely home,
and for the time that's left to us,
you'll have no need to roam."

The wanderer, he settles down
before the fire, sighs,
and stretches out, and licks each hand,
then closes his old eyes.

ONE-SIDED CONVERSATION WITH THE COVID-19 CORONAVIRUS (with apologies to Dr. Seuss)

I do not like you, COVID v.
I do not like you, so you see
I wish that you would go away—
don't come again another day.
I do not like you, this is true
because the only thing you do
is make us sick and disrupt lives
of friends and families, husbands, wives.

You make us stay inside when we
have lots of things to do and see.
You make us hoard hand sanitizers,
and turn us into greedy misers
piling toilet-paper rolls
into closets, hidey-holes.
We're doing social distancing,
have turned to online conferencing,
but I don't like this way of being
or all the tragedy I'm seeing.
So I'll repeat myself to say:
COVID-19, go away!

Maria Berardi

ZOOM

When I am listening
looking at these faces
      I feel how we are all together.

It is when I speak that the space
shouts out where I am,
      off-kilter, vertiginous, alone.

ORIGIN STORY
for Rosemerry Wahtola Trommer

Robert Burn's love is like a red, red rose,
and you wrote that your love is like a rabbitbrush.

I like that: tenacious, common, canny.
For one thing to be like another thing, a simile:

my love is like a red, red rose,
my love is like rabbitbrush.

The actual enters
in the thin sticks of letters.

A simile is a picture, useful;
a metaphor is an invocation,

incantation, incarnation;
real, and dangerous,

a spell,
a conception.

Auden said, "Poetry makes nothing happen."
I say, poetry makes Nothing, *happen*,

calls forth the Something
in the Nothing and brings it

to birth in this world,
And so we do no less.

Judyth Hill

COVID KINTSUGI

"Kintsugi, 'golden joinery' is a Japanese technique that repairs broken pottery using gold applied with lacquer; and a philosophy: that breakage and repair are part of the history of an object, not something to disguise."
~ Lauren Miller, *Words of Women*

Chant 108 Sacred Names
for Beloveds gone, scatter rose petals.
Call everyone you love

Because

This road leads straight to the hearth.
What do we pack to stay home?
Build an Altar to the old Ordinary:

packed movie theatres, *Stormy Weather* and *The Producers*
cappuccino in cafés, dance class.
All past loves, forgiven, because really,

why not? Collect all we miss: haircuts, nights on the town,
icy margs at the crowded bar. Opening Day
at the Ballpark, beach shack feasts. Old Bay on everything.

Reaching for the hand of a stranger in greeting,
the long line at the post office, moving slow but good conversation.
Inviting a friend over for tea, leaning in for a kiss.

Every door closed means you get to see the room you are already in.
What if Here is enough? And Now?
How everything fell, a crazy Icarus, into the sea.

Disappearing work, restaurants,
parades, dropping in for a visit.
So fragile our expectations/hopes/needs!

How dissolve and melt ensued!
There goes habit! Jobs! Routines origami into

afternoons watching bread rise, turning pages,

checking email again and again.
Oh, rinse of Repeat! Hours and hours of News.
Black is the new black.

So much loss and solitude, looking like a kitchen and lots of time.

Say prayers for the many.
Light candles. Bless wine,
break bread.

Soon we each will have lost someone.
Soon. Tell their stories;
make their name for a Blessing.

Because

What could open? Our hearts.
What can we give without touch? Love.
What can we send without postage? Prayers.
What is ever Present? Beauty.

Breath by breath, we do these slow days.
These days do us, set on Rerun,
coffee, news, stack wood, tea.

Punctuated by snacks, snacks, snacks.

Who makes pancakes for 1? Gluten free no less?
Rise to the occasion and shore up your courage: offer hope, hilarity,
        chutzpah!
Stockpile patience.

As plans fall away, the Moon answers.
The open palm of the Divine is offered as lists are unmade,
What if? and *When?* and the answer, you know,

is, *Who Knows?*
This might be the slowdown that saves!
The Open Door to Dream!

Take the B train, baby, crosstown, where your quiet lives.

We invent a new intimacy
born of eyes shining kindness
above a fancy/plain/simple/elaborate mask.

My mask a gift to you, yours a gift to me: collateral care.

Last night, I had company:
the moon, in her crescent self, and maybe Venus.
Shining in unbidden! Planets ignore social distance,

cross borders unmasked. Not me,
I'm masked Fashionista, in 'jamas, glitter eyeliner.
Mask as Next Frontier! Get radical! ¡Qué viva!

Shift the Culture from v I r to Us

The heart has signposts – tracing the way,
Virtual is the new Love Language.
Masked, we'll cross safely to New.

Kintsugi.

We'll turn Broken into Mend: the gold of hold,
the heal of seal.
The parts our lives broke into, reset.

 We'll let the rejoined edges shine.

Apply the resilient skin of solve, patch of Peace,
move forward into what we do not,
cannot know. But Home,

is where the story starts.
The view of startling hillside in May snow,
insects flitting in the late lit air.

Deer at the salt block, hummingbird at sweet
Click and hush, soar, a buzzing roar.

Aspens leafing tender, just barely out.

Here's no alone, just, a day,
lived breath by breath.
Light through pine forest, deer at dusk, Mama fox and her kits,
bounding loop de loop in the meadow. Contagious joy!

Because

This tells our rhizomic truth.
Spread the Word: we were always Going Viral!
So many ways that apart: we gather. A part,

we are whole.

Sandra S. McRae

DICE CUP

Just now, when you read this poem's title, you heard that rattle, the loaded potential of luck, good or bad. For me it's a flashback to games with my siblings or grandmother while Mom prepared dinner, finally undisturbed. How petty now those pangs of jealousy every time my best friend yelled *Yahtzee!*, since she would be dead by age 36.

My friend Murray told me ravens have their own language, over 30 distinct sounds. One of them he calls "dice cup." Every day I walk up the mountain, listening for that elusive call, hoping to glean its meaning from whatever circumstance might inspire it. I've hiked thousands of miles, but I've only heard it a couple times, from afar.

Years ago, a colleague told me of watching his father die— the labored wheezing, then a rasping struggle that lasted longer than he could bear, before a final sigh, then peace.

My mother died of the coronavirus. My brother followed the ambulance to the hospital, where she was whisked away, never to be seen or touched by us again. Now all I have is the movie that started when the nurse tried to explain the chain of events that morning. This after a three-week battle she seemed to have won—at least that's what the tests said. I ran the movie backward to the last time I saw her, laughing and smiling across the dinner table. I thought I could stay with that happily-before-the-ever-after but the movie leaps off the screen to roar in my face with its toxic spittle.

Nowhere does the sound of death match your imagination. The good dog I let off the leash pounced on the chipmunk's back. There was a silent writhing, a tiny mouth opened, and the little chipmunk soul left the body as the breeze fluffed its soft animal fur. Years later we watched the dog, after all that ragged panting, finally relax and lean back. As her head slipped off her bed, her ear slowly flopped open, like a flower blossoming. None of us breathed as we watched the light ascend.

After my mother died, a certain raven followed me every day as I pounded up the mountain as fast as I could, stomping out my grief since tears refused to materialize. I don't know what my mother thought as she fought for breath that wouldn't come.

I have yet to decipher the dice cup call of the raven. I don't know what receptors lie furled in the curls of a dog's tender nose, or the millions of chemical exchanges that transpire there at lightning speed as we tug on the leash, insisting: "Come on! We gotta go."

ADVANCE COPY OF EULOGY

Standing in the dim basement storeroom
I survey my future inheritance from my mother:

Rows and rows of canned goods
arranged by contents and brands.
A motley collection of florist shop vases
from Daddy's funeral in 1976.
A dusty assortment of retired suitcases
that never lived up to their potential.
Clear plastic totes stuffed with worn
Christmas decorations
preserved for sentimental
rather than cosmetic appeal.
A ceramic Santa cookie jar
painted by a neighbor who moved away
decades ago.
A crystal candy dish
of unknown origin.
The square tub she stores the pizzelles in.
Nested serving platters
employed at five weddings
one baby shower
countless Sunday dinners.

I stand alone
feeling all there is to lose
until Mom hollers from the kitchen:
What's taking you so long?
It's time to add the tomatoes.

MAMA!

He called your name
as the last breath left him
as the full weight of the state
bore down on his neck
and the sharp pebbles of indifference
pressed up into his throat.
He called out to you
with his last wisp of strength—

surely he saw your sweet face
lined with worry
the worn paths of concern you tread
every time he left the house
a young man of promise
bouncing on the balls of his feet
eager to get out into the world.

A man is a man is a man

until a brute comes along
and kneels on his throat
for 8
    minutes
    46
    seconds.

Mama! he cried
Mama—save me—

and now his voice
is in the ears
of all the mamas

his name is on our lips

we will not stop screaming
until all brutes who kneel
are brought to heel.

Robert Cooperman

THE SPHINX'S RIDDLE

Setting out on our morning walk,
I take the cane I keep by the door,
and it strikes me—as I'd like to strike
idiots mesmerized by their Delphic cellphones—

that I could answer the Sphinx's riddle
fast as Oedipus did, but would graciously refuse
Thebes' kingship, never a monarchist,
especially now, a certain person thinking
he's royalty, everyone else losers to lie to
that everything's great, or bully into silence.

What goes on four legs in the morning,
two at noon, and three in the evening?

The answer obvious now, but in mythic Greece
so many travelers got it wrong, or froze,
and were eaten by that half lion, half woman
who guarded the mountain pass into Thebes.

I'd pose as her descendant and put the question
to him, instead of those five words he claimed
he remembered, as if blessed with an eidetic memory.
When he'll look panicked, can't think metaphorically—
never having read a novel or seen a Greek tragedy—
he'll shrivel and vanish into a piss-aromatic puddle,

just like the Wicked Witch of the West.

THE GRASS CURE

When my brother visited
a few years back, he complained
of foot pain gnawing
like a small vicious rodent,
his doctor, back in New York,
unable to figure out why.

"Maybe you should try some pot,"
I suggested, weed legal here,
the dispensary a block away.

"Can't hurt," he shrugged;
we walked, slowly, to the shop,
the owner more a sommelier—
offering us a sniff, and extolling
the virtues and properties
of each blend he brought out—
than the back-in-the-day dealers
who wore shades,
carried more weaponry
than a small town police force,
and might try to pass off oregano
or dried ficus blades for the real thing.

At home, we toked up.
A few minutes later, I asked
how his foot was doing: laughter
loud and raucous as a murder of crows.

"So the grass is working?" I smiled.

"Nope, still hurts like a mother fucker,"
Jeff guffawed at the best joke ever,
"but right now, who cares?"

DNA TESTING

They say not to swab the side
of your mouth and send the sample in
if you're not prepared to be surprised:
like Bill, whose grandmother swore
the family was pure English stock.

"No damn drunken Irish in our blood!"
her rant, never a drop of Bushmills
or Guinness sullied her lips or her husband's,
though he'd wanted to be a bartender;
but she'd cut him with a glare Carrie Nation
might've envied before taking her ax to a keg.

So of course Bill laughed when he found
more Irish ancestry than English, and more
Native American than both combined:
everyone's dream nowadays, to claim kin
with Geronimo, Cochise, and Crazy Horse,
and feel more righteous than descendants
of the Mayflower or the Jamestown Colony.

Me? I've always assumed Cossack-
rapist blood swirled somewhere in my DNA,
but never cared enough to find out.

As for Bill, he chuckles every time
he thinks of his grandmother.

"She'd twist in her grave if she knew,"
he wipes his eyes over our bi-weekly
pizza lunch. "Even worse," he chortles,
"if she knew there were Italian genes
mixed up in the soup," and takes a big,
smiling bite of the Margherita special.

HENRY AND THE FBI

Neighbors called him, "Devilish Henry,"
driving his parents nuts, tormenting
his little brother Leonard: once,
hogtying him and hoisting his small,
squirming body upside down
onto a neighbor's doorknob,
then ringing the bell and hiding,
almost peeing himself with laughter.

Mrs. Sloan dragged open the door
strangely heavy as a Mack Truck
and gasped: Leonard, mortified,
ran when she freed him.
Another time, Henry wrote to J. Edgar Hoover
in grade-school-block-letters,
that he wanted to be an FBI agent.

"I'll stop drinking and go to church
every Sunday if I can work for the greatest
man in history," and signed Leonard's name.
Two weeks later, the phone detonated:
a man with a motorcycle-cop voice
demanded to speak to Leonard Kelly.

"Do you think we'd accept a drunkard?"
his irony-free voice rasping with threats
of prison beatings, for wasting the FBI's time.

"I'm ten years old and I never wrote any letter,"
Leonard stammered; and dropped the phone
as if it were a crazed, scratching cat,
their father motioning to Henry,
uncoiling his belt.

PERPETUAL CARE

A letter from the cemetery where Mom's buried
offers perpetual care for a sum roughly equivalent
to the National Debt: to forever keep her plot clean
as the kitchen floor she swept after every meal.

After I stop fuming about how the cemetery uses
grief and guilt, I wonder if I shouldn't pay: how much
longer will I be able to make Seasonal Care payments?

Beth's parents' ashes were spread around the base
of a Colorado peak they loved to live under,
two stones erected in the town's tumbleweed graveyard.
When Beth and I visit, she speaks softly to her parents;
I place pebbles atop their monuments, though neither
was a Jew, just my sign of respect, of love.

The last time we visited my mother's New York stone,
and talked to her as if we'd stopped by for tea and cookies,
my aunt complained to the front office that despite
our seasonal care checks, the plot was overgrown
with weeds, leaves caught like mice in traps
in the untrimmed shrubbery that should've made the plot
look like a blanket for a peaceful sleeper.

So I tear up the letter, since let's face it, no one's
here forever to take care of family business,
but how I want to call my mother right now, to find out
how she's doing, and if they're treating her okay.

THE CHRISTMAS THIEF

I tried to keep down the Don Corleone voice
rasping in my head that I wasn't going home,
the wife and kids better off without me,
when I aimed my gas belching dragon
to the smart side of town, past sleeping cops
in their black-and-whites, after free meals
at a local diner, taking extra pies for later.

I picked the house with a display lit up
so bright, space aliens could spot it.
At one basement window, I used the barrel
of the piece I'd bought off Tommy Lockhart,
muffled the sound by wrapping the gun
in a pillow case, then snuck upstairs
to the chandeliered dining room
and under my Trump mask, barked,

"Everything in here!" and flipped open
the pillow case like a magician;
the women shrieked, the men sullen
as little kids told they'd have to miss
their favorite shows; one pretty, over-painted
and jeweled number stared and hissed.

"Take me too, I'm so freaking bored!"

"You got no idea how good you got it,"
I copped a feel, and was gone, to where,
maybe Satan knew, but neither me nor Jesus
had a clue: my wife and kids waiting
for daddy to make the holidays sparkle.

Gerard Smaldone

I LOOK AT POETRY AS AN AFFLICTION
(MaryKay Smaldone)

When you are young
the duende is beaten into you

the devil does his work
leaves an indelible mark
burnished on your soul

But as you age, it's pounded out,
crumbles into dust, devoured by time.

And an angel, just as carefully
rubs the pain and longing out,

memory fades, as he goes
about his labors, day and night.

At some point, you catch him
smiling slyly, waiting patiently
to see if you get the joke.

For the mark still shines
even more brightly, and where
you thought it had disappeared

your desire for death and all
the mysteries she leads you to
overcomes you like a shadow

makes you question again every
thought and feeling you cannot own,
though they are supposedly yours.

No, they belong to the impenetrable night

of impossibilities that call from hidden corners

in a voice that cruelly begs, then softly
sings, and the day has its own rules
that it barely understands

and you wait for the end
with a sense of hopeless faith
in the doors she will will open

an innocent donkey sacrificed to
the empty rooms of the Self

and the Nameless that fills them
with your infinite tears and fevered life.

for Ken Greenley

Jared Smith

SOMEHOW THE SOUL STILL SOARS

Birds fly heavy in the evening.
No songs to sing. No worms to catch.
Just the long trip homeward over
fields and houses and empty highways.
The great blue heron ghostly gray
soaring its way into shadows over
its mirrored estuary farm pond,
over the tall grasses, the reeds
that bend in the wind, the trails
only those of tooth and claw follow.
He has dipped his mouth in the mud
of our cities and feasted on frogs, eels,
salamanders, and ancient decay.
His wingspan is immense in our time.

Time covers everything.
The city of Minneapolis is burning tonight.
The law has placed its knee on a man's throat.
The cities of Denver and of Los Angeles burn..
More than one hundred fifty years gone by
and white sheets have been placed everywhere
men struggle to support their families in cities,
in fields and houses and empty highways
in the shadows mirrored over farm ponds
where the souls of men still somehow soar
time covers everything that bends in the winds.

Carol Guerrero-Murphy

ODE TO THE FUTURE IN THIS PANDEMIC (A PANTOUM)

You've never actually been there, Future, only a gloved finger
    beckoning,
a partner for a waltz we never learn how to lead or follow,
blue crocus underground and snow geese wintering in the south,
no part of you more than a wish or a prayer, faithless lover.

A partner for a waltz I never learned to lead or follow,
you're a dancer wearing a gown spun of milk jugs and cornstarch
    shoes.
You've never been more than a ten-cent prayer, faithless,
scribed on paper and burned in winter, a summery green ash rising.

A dancer in a gown of milk-jug silk and flimsy shoes
you won't be recognized when you arrive. It will be today,
scribed on burning paper, summery green ash rising
even though I saw you, our Future running away.

We won't recognize you when you arrive. It will be today.
What could you do to remind me I invited you to breakfast
(I saw you, hair streaming, running away)
when you come now in your goggles and smothered grin?

Could you remind me I invited you to breakfast,
blue crocus underground and spring geese restless, muttering in the
    south?
You approach now in goggles and secret smile.
You've never actually been here, a gloved finger beckoning.

ZOOMING WITH THE HORSE AND 7 VARIATIONS

1.
In profile, Horse shifts his dark
windowed eye a little down
and to the left to say scratch that
pull off that burr or tick
and I can't see what it is, never
will know, anyway no chance
to pull it off, scratch
and after all he's dead
as my vet said zooming in horse heaven
his sky legs regained.

2.
In Time Lapse Zoom, your tulips bud, open wider, show their
throats.

3.
Zooming with the rabbit, She
turns one ear back then her head follows, then
there is only her rear and that tell-tale tail.

4.
I never get Roadrunner on the schedule to zoom.
Too fast for me.

5.
Zooming with your dogs, they get so close
I can read their brains through their noses,
all their thoughts breathing out
until they speak alternately saying
throw the ball or *where's the ball* or
here's the ball, then zoom away.

6.
My sister writes about watching lizards
doing pushups on their fairy tale fingers
and if she zooms me

they too will have a chance to zoom under a stone.

7.
In Time Lapse Zoom marigold petals drop
and drift like snow
Then snow.

8.
I never see it coming, the sadness.
Right when I am laughing to think of zooming
the horse, the rabbit, the lizard, tulip, dogs—
might as well be fishes below a skin of lake
too deep to reach and if
I should net one out somehow
to stream my fingertip across her silver slick side,
and took her home with me
she would likely die.
So with you in the time of La 'Rona,
friend zooming Safer Far Away, seen
not even through a glass but pixelated in some way,
not really seen at all. Imagined.

Padma Thornlyre

REMEMBERING LAURA MAZE AND DONNA JEAN AS THE SAME WOMAN

Let affections be afflictions, I say, nympholeptic seizures
over the delicately-sequined dress she's wearing,
on the other side of the sky, as Patchen sd,
and the articulation of fishnet, its hint
at the flex and quiver of calf and three-dimensionality.
Undressing her a disappointment; this time, frankly,
it's the package that stirs the reflective urge,
the outline of self in all its objectivity.

Ah, the different places I see her!—
dressed the same, seated in the same posture—
at a barstool, alone, off to the right in Hopper's Nighthawks,
at the Niçoise in downtown Denver
her Sapphire martini straight up and dirty.
I see her in cottonwood branches thus,
and perched on the power-lines overhead,
and in the bowl of the crescent moon like the gauzy girl
we all wd know who lounges in the Maxfield Parish-ish
Belle Epoch poster hanging in someone else's living room,
cheaply framed under cracked glass, but prominently
displayed. Her she sits on a closed toilet seat, smoking.
Not that she smoked in the flesh, or maybe she did
and I never knew. I just don't know.
But here she is, smoking, seated on porcelain,
wearing sequins.

I've had my loves, and now a seven-year marriage—
a first date that never ended. This isn't the seven-year
itch, but may there always be room for loves unrequited,
the sweetness of a fruit never tasted,
never more perfectly ripe

than when thinking of it now. Each now. Yes, let Beauty now
and then remain suspended, a mnemonic device:
there she sits sequined, bobbing on the green pony
on the carousel; and there, sequined and weightless
in fishnets, she rides the red curve of a Calder
in something less wind than breath.

CHINA CAT
for Reven Marie Swanson

1.
I've grown accustomed
to her rough, hollow back,

the glaze upon her nude
torso, her belly slightly

rounded, even the bullet
holes in her armpit and neck,

holes too perfectly, lovingly
round to be aught else, their

precision so clean, so
business-like, and so

eloquently matter-of-fact.
Holes where I've placed

a blossom or two—sunflower,
bird of paradise, thistle

gathered with gloves.
I've hung my hat on her

ceramic head, and now
and then ran a finger over

the underside of those lovely,
lopsided breasts, tickling

down to an outward jut, a
suggestion of womanly hips.

2. *(an aside)*
In Circe's eyes blue
Krishna lies, upon her black
lashes Radha sighs.

3.
They tumble, all three of them, a
menagerie of hips, buttocks, breasts

and thighs—roundnesses we seldom
see in our hard-body world—neo-

paleolithic apparitions dript by lunatic
barklight. Could I enter their dark

I would, I'd be the wind that wafts
them, the bed of reeds they rest upon.

4. *(an aside)*
the Gopi's milkpails
are full but weightless and float
upon his piping

5.
An egg in glass suspended gluts
the mid-air; nearby, a glass bird

more *Damoiselle d'Avignon*
than whippoorwill, is,

though motionless,
no less melodious.

6. *(an aside)*
soft-soled, and my abs

well-disguised; my olding beard
alone redeems me.

7.
A pomegranate broken by hand,
and shared, a drum, a toke, merlot,

a hot garlic bulb to spread on warm
bread, one toke and then another,

a cold marble flank to caress,
smoother than skin, and longer living.

8. *(an aside)*
The best tamales I've ever
eaten, red or green,
are served up by Oszy,

a gruff-talking whitebeard
Deadhead, from his
shiny white van with two

bright red, neon chili pepper
signs secured to the roof,
right here in Evergreen,

across from the library on
Highway 73; and I buy my
favorite jerky, too (buffalo, elk)

from another old hippie who parks
his beat-up brown van in Clear
Creek, next canyon over.

9.
Bordered by the memory of sage and laurel—
leaves from your private garden

kilned to mere imprint, and discarded ash—
a ram-horned man, or god, and slightly

above him, She, round and brown,
donning moonlight like chiffon.

10. *(an aside)*
Seven honks at 6 a.m.
echoed by a crow's six cries.
O, for the slingshot

and sure aim of my youth!—
the stones for the human, mind you,

not for the augur of autumn.

My wife does not awaken;
my daughter coughs,
as she has for five weeks,

but otherwise doesn't stir.
Only I am wide-eyed,
resigned and sighing for coffee.

11.
Yes, I would see myself mirrored,
splintered and fragmented, even

such breasts are comforting—
the shape of meditation, a mandala.

12. *(an aside)*
Silly Girl!

13.
stone, glass, charcoal, self-
quarried Yule marble,

laurel-leaf and sage-leaf,
kiln and glaze, your knobs

on the cupboard doors
and sweet smoke & all

the world is acute, piercing
the thin blue, our breath

suddenly heavy, this
blustering chinook wind

a light, electric flicker
up and down the spine.

Lisa Zimmerman

ABOVE AND BELOW IN THE 21st CENTURY

Under the city
        dinosaur bones.
Under the city
        ash of our ancestors.
Under the city, unspeakable and fragile: sorrow
        ground down into powder, war
        crushed into sand.
Above the city
        flat blue ocean of sky—
        flat blue gasp of forgiveness.

ANOTHER FULL YEAR

The bud is humming
In the marrow of the branch
Leaves green my sleeping

One blue dragonfly
Glides above the grassy path
Far rumor of rain

Wind rips through dry corn
Trees crack, unlatch their hinges
Leaf scraps everywhere

Sparrows picking seeds
Snow's armor brightens the field
Cold sun a white knife

Jon Kelly Yenser

TIME FOR EVERYTHING
> "Are you looking for a screws and bolts set?"
> —Amazon

On a gloomy day I was sorting nails
from screws from metal do-dads
saved over decades and rattling
now at the bottom of a toolbox
with cantilevered trays—what one buys
to organize once and for all
all the drill bits, drivers and hammers
of several sizes so he can find
what's needed when the garden gate
swells to such a weight with rain water
you can't drag it shut. It was midday

and sunny and I was sitting in the shade
of the pergola, picking things over,
pushing one way or the other
everything with a point.   About the swollen gate:
I thought most of us, if we give it
any thought, will simply unhinge it
and plane the bottom edge.
That way you can leave the nails
and screws, the do-dads and brass plates
in the toolbox for the estate sale,
one more unsorted lot.

INVATION OF THE MOTHS

Never saw anything like this.
Nothing to do with the virus
in all likelihood just another
thing about nature we don't get.
This evening's dust gathering
in a corner of the living room ceiling,
I step up, trying to balance
on the sofa, swatting with a tea towel,
guessing at spots.
    I think of dancing
curveballs I never had a chance
of hitting on the sandlot. I set
my feet, dig in, swing, miss.
Look at us: age and balance
moths and virus. Never like this.

ON RTE. 66

What kind of chickenshit calls the cops on a couple of speeders? I mean really. They're at least 2 blocks away, on old 66, a pair of then with glass packs or something louder.

I did. Now that I am old and cranky. In the old days, though,.

Back on the North side in Wichita this was unacceptable behavior, of course.

And in their defense, these two yahoos probably don't have much else to do. The Virus and all has shut the breweries down. The taverns. Most of the cafes, not that these guys drink coffee or munch gateaux. But still.

What kind of chickenshit calls the cops on drag racers?

The cops don't want to come out. For speeders? Really? Who knows where the kids have been, what kind of social proximity they have been practicing every chance they get. Which, as I say, is not much probably.

Now that the busses aren't running, they got all kinds of room on the main drag.

The cops don't want to come out at all. Besides the speeders are, almost certainly, white kids. The brown kids don't go speeding. They dress up their sedans and drop them to the ground and make them bounce, make them sway. Those lowriders know shit from shinola.

And the black kids don't have cars that go fast.

And the Navaho kids. Well, there you go.

What kind of chickenshit calls the cops?

Veronica Patterson

MY GRANDCHILD
"Walk into the time that is coming."
—Jane Hirshfield

Last night, climbing the stairs
from the basement
to read and maybe sleep
despite the sick ache of a world
that cannot breathe,
I came face to face with a rabbit
at the glass back door. Like
images in the virus news, this
could be a grandchild visiting
a grandmother, a thick pane
between them. We looked long.
I have no grandchild
but there you were.

I have books I could read to you:
Peter Rabbit, *The Country Bunny
and the Little Gold Shoes*, *Watership
Down* when you're older, that book
of a world destroyed, flight, courage,
mistakes, a world to rebuild, luck.
"Rabbit rabbit," I say first thing on
the first day of each month,
a childhood ritual for luck.
I would never want your foot
to carry in my pocket.

There are foxes here, I want
to tell you, a large hawk, though
I can't protect you. Is the world
weakening? Darkening? Let's
go softly now to curl in separate
sleeps. I'll dream how to act on
our behalf, for the sake of this earth,

on which our kin may still thrive when
you and I are gone from under the sun,
under the moon. I touch the glass
and your ears twitch forward.
I ask, What time is it? for you,
for me, this place.

MEDITATION ON THIS AUTUMN
After reading John Keats' "To Autumn" in 2020

1. When everything hurts. When everything's hurt. The fires shocking, the dry fuel load abundant. Our daughters too far away and justice farther. Or further, my English teacher would have said, because it's not actual distance. Or is it? Flames in mountain forests, in the cities, in the soul. Season of mists, John Keats wrote, not meaning smoke. The maturing sun rises red with warning. Will it fill all fruits with ripeness? Apples pressed to cider. We, hard-pressed to the core where fear lies. Almost no peaches with their rose-gold smell of *yes*, of flesh, their plump furred curves. Barred clouds linger above gold fields; we have not brought in the sheaves.

2. But a crop of unsleeved arms rises like stalks of wheat, row upon row in waves, in the streets of place after place—for justice we haven't sown deep enough to reap. Some fists, like buds, want to open. But don't breathe. Corona, a resonant word for what crowns the careless and the careful and the caring, cutting swaths to sorry stubble across this land, across this world, across unready hearts. And mourning kin become a wailful choir.

3. I walk into morning black-masked, wanting to gather what I see— the green pumpkin pondering orange, zucchini escaped from garden into gutter. Clusters of grapes, half green, half purpled. At home, in the kitchen, the ripening cantaloupe reaches for me with its heady scent of near-readiness; juice and seeds flood the inner gloom. Patience, no one says; nevertheless, I make tea. Then, on the bottom of the wild-rose painted cup I rinse, a tiny rose, open wide, a later flower.

4. Blown, the rose blown open, like a heart.

IT IS THE SWALLOWS

knit me a loose scarf of their flights

>—walking by the river
>during the pandemic

It is the swallows console
me, their interwoven swooping,

catching insects. Arc upon arc,
they etch morning. Flights

crisscross above the river,
an emulsion of swallows, air

and insects, immiscible, yet this
exact mix consoles me. A sudden

village of mud huts burgeons
under the bridge overhang, each

a thousand pellets, and in this
gypsy encampment, hatchlings

poke tiny wide-open beaks into a river
of air. They will be fed.

Marcia Jones

PASSIONATE PILGRIM
> "Fight for the things that you care about."
> —Ruth Bader Ginsburg

Tonight stars and stripes tremble
in September breezes, red,
white, and blue at half-mast
      against a black sky of mourning.

Light glows behind white pillars
of justice at the Supreme Court.
We gather in darkness and light
      grieving for you, American hero.

A woman of firsts, tiny pioneer,
you rise tall for justice. Fervent feminist,
your voice rings to transform our world
      echoes in this night of loss.

Death cannot steal your spirit.
Passionate pilgrim, we hold your hand
on our long path toward equality
      tired and dusty, we keep walking.

LEAVE THE BALCONY OPEN
"If I die, leave the balcony open."
—Federico Garcia Lorca

Just today,
will you leave the balcony open?

I want to feel the sun sift
through the shutter slats
and slowly stripe the covers
rustled on my bed

. . . touch the day's fever
one more time, smell
its sensual, faint scorch,
stroking, warming my skin

. . . look through the black railing,
laced with dust and last pots
of summer flowers, red petals
withering, waning

. . . listen to cool whispers
of a serene breeze tracing
my face, soothing bad dreams,
chasing forgotten memories

. . . reflect on mislaid desire,
lost in labyrinths of regret,
remember the way we danced
when we couldn't imagine an end

. . . wait for twilight's birdsong,
timeless slants of light when my spirit
will take wing through these open doors
into blue blue endlessness.

But, if I long for one more day,
will you leave the balcony open
tomorrow?

YELLOW SKY

The West burns hot. Charred trees
rise in silhouettes against enraged
yellow skies. Smoke smothers
endangered neighborhoods.

A pandemic stalks fired towns.
Restless protests seethe and churn.
Politicians shout lies from bully pulpits.
We try to talk with one another.

Yellow skies twist to tangerine. Fire rains
until we drown in sparks of silent dread.
Today we remember those who leaped
in orange skies from blazing towers.

And lately, too many friends stare
malignancy in his yellow face.
Too many sink in pain and despair,
hiding helpless behind black masks.

Skies will shine blue again. But now,
they writhe in smoke to crimson.
Fire-etched mountains light the horizon,
tragic beauty in the horror.

Peggy Knoepfle

senior living

here I am
in a strange university
where everyone majors
in dying
but the extra-curricular activities
are more important
than the degree

we've gone skinny
gotten giddy and a little wild
like the teenagers we were
so long ago
hello high school
our bodies are changing
and no one knows
what the next hour will bring

Lon Wartman

LYNCHING

Black man floating in space
Knotted rope about his face
Crosses burning
White sheets chanting

Black man squirming
Blue knee choking
Buildings burning
Dark nights looming

A noose from a tree
A boot and a knee
A black man dead
No one led

Gutters vomiting
Jesus faltering
Canisters of tears
Scattering fears

Memories from the past
Recall the last
Nothing changed
Our nation estranged

Horrible brutality
Watching reality
A hang man's stage
Millions enraged

Dusty roads
A hang man's noose
Burning streets
A black man pleading

So much the same

It's just insane
Equal justice
No longer trusted

Civil unrest
A nation stressed
Yet we care
When tempers flare

Doing it right
With all our might
We must listen
As rattlesnakes hissen

It begins in the mind
You learn to be kind
We are all blood inside
Where love resides

It is not right
That I am white
And am not black
But my soul is cracked

I FEEL YOUR PAIN . . . .
As George was slain
I watched it all
His terrible fall

Again and Again
Again and Again

A henchman calling
A nation bleeding

Again and Again
Again and Again

Crosses burning
Mindsets never learning
It was a lynching

Kyle Laws

THE LILACS ARE GONE

Banded black and white neck of the woodpecker
erect with military bearing
as it struts the yard
bends to the ground over off-shoots
in the pale dust of winter brushed with ice.

Each spring lilacs budded to a deceptive sun
were wrestled to the ground in snow
the first week of May
as if the house were dealing a hand of cards
no one could win with and you still kept betting.

THE ANGLE OF THINGS

In a boat across rapids,
I bail the bottom of leavings.

Silence is not enough to hold
the tension in a drop of water.

A BREAK TO HEAL

Super moon, once in a blue moon, blood moon,
I amble out onto the back porch
even though dangerous,
even though dawn seems uncertain,
even though nothing may ever be the same.

The mind cannot will a break to heal,
cannot spin a web around roses to prevent the fade,
going from a blood rivulet that runs down glass
to what is dried and withered and folded around bud.
What remains is past redemption.

WHO HEARD THE SUNSET YOWL?

The sun set bloody on the bay
a wound open to a shuffle of feet
on the sand on the street
march of the same shoes
in evening

that do not tread the beach
do not enter the rough and tumble
of tide that leaves what's trapped
in tendrils of seaweed
no longer heading to sea

but wrapped in an envelope
without wax and seal
so it returns and returns
the sand a brown of tea
stains that can't be scrubbed

without bleach
smell more foreign than clams
broken and the bloat of fish
with hook in a jaw of teeth
so be careful

across the lip of wave
in the drop that recedes
the breath taken and held
blood silent and mean
on an isthmus.

Frank Coons

GRAPPLING WITH A BIT OF ASTROPHYSICS AND THE OPTIMUM WRINKLE CREAM

> "What a piece of work is man."
> —William Shakespeare

It was for a time, a gnawing hunger,
to know for the sake of knowing
what was beyond the beyond,
what was inside every inside, how cats purr,
and if we are alone in the universe.

It was for the sheer joy of exploring
the rings of Saturn, the why
of the dog star and the red eye
of Jupiter with all those moons watching.
It was inventing compostable toilets.

It was, of course, time itself
and its avatar, space
It was a single molecule of helium,
and who makes the best chicken sandwich,
the god particle, and black holes

It was answers without questions and a bright
& carnal species constrained by gravity,
toying with nuclear physics, the optimum
wrinkle cream, interstellar travel.

URSA MINOR OR WHATEVER THE OPPOSITE OF CHEVALIER IS

Some Sundays
I hold in myself something
of the bear,
confined and solitary,
circling for continuous calories,
erratic sleep habits.
And I devolve.
My back grows hair
and my words go monosyllabic
as I repair into my deep hidden
dark midden, a *Man Cave*.

Behold the reliquary
of tarnished sports trophies,
lacquered plaques from various
bowling allies,
a fridge full of beer,
cheap neon bar signs
for Jim Beam or Guinness,
where Big Billy Bass
sings "take me to the river"—
every time I ask,

a sacristy centered
around an old divan
and a *Lazy Boy* that fit
my lumbering frame
to a T and the giant TV
won't allow *Downton Abbey*
or *Antiques Road Show*
to despoil my manly space,
where manly games grace
the overlarge screen,
and I score my points vicariously.

Michael Henry

NUMBERS AND FIGURES

it's still early and my wife is upstairs
talking to some people on Zoom
our 2 girls are huddled
on the couch
under a blanket
the dog has been in and out
47 times so far today

it feels cold inside
but the heat is set to 71
I am
54 years old
actually that is
wrong I am
only 53

it's been a week of inside
all the time
outside the remnant of
yesterday's snowstorm
is still so white yet
melting into itself
as the chariot of the sun
runs its arcing path

yes our 2 old friends
hope and warmth are
with us now but
like always they're going to
fade away
they say another storm
is soon to come
at 3 AM
when we are asleep

my friend Chris is gone
it's been over 4 months now
I think of him
at least 3 times a day
and there are 2
open bottles of scotch on top
of the 1 fridge
we have 6 trees
in our back yard
which to me is
4 too many but
my wife likes them
it's the green and the oxygen
the Oh 2

how many days this
inside living will remain
is anyone's guess
solve for x
no one has
scribbled an equation
on a chalkboard
or yellow notepad

numbers are cold
so certain of themselves
they tally everything yet
so much
slips past
their high self-esteem

today is 1 day
tomorrow will be
1 also
this is all I can say
for sure right now

ANDY WARHOL'S SILVER CLOUDS
for Em and Sue

Silver balloons float in a dark room
and many kids are in there.
A couple have been broken, burst by boys,
deconstructing the art installation.

A gang of kids are in there, hands outstretched.
The balloons are more like pillows.
My choice of noun deconstructs the installation.
The tag says Andy Warhol made them.

The balloons are more like pillows,
and I want to go in there, and I want to leave.
The tag says Andy Warhol made them—
not these exact pillows, just the idea of them,

and I want to go home, I want to call my sister,
I want my daughter to not have a boyfriend,
not this exact boyfriend, any boyfriend.
She's too young to be sick, my sister.

I want my daughter not to have a boyfriend,
she's too young to have one, my little girl.
She's too young to be sick, my sister.
The balloons, unbroken, float and glimmer.

She's too young to have a boyfriend, my little girl.
She should be playing tennis with other girls.
The balloons float and glimmer.
She should find a muse in her own bones.

She should be alone or with friends who are girls.
Boys are too rough—they're breaking the silver pillows.
My sister should be a muse for her own bones,
My daughter's room should be full of silver pillows.

POEM BEGINNING WITH LINES FROM BOB DYLAN

In the room the heat pipes just cough
and the country music station plays soft,
and I cannot find anything to turn off,
so when the film projector jams
I am too late. That sad burn-and-peel
of the home movie lives I once knew—
my first two-wheeled bike ride,
my sisters and I leaping into a pool,
or, before my time, Mom and Dad's
after-wedding dash to a green car
tailed with stringed cans,
all in a faded Kodachrome field.
The celluloid has bubbled and smoked
away and broke, leaving me
to wander white blaze with whirring fan.
How strange as each dawn the sky
turns blue and I'm reminded of the dead
cold mornings when I used to pray
for the earth to let me go.
Now I pray I will have all the time
I'll need, before I'm found again
in the tiny wood-paneled rooms
of the old house on McKinley Parkway
as those old pipes cough and clank,
where country music plays soft, twangy
and sweet on an old radio somewhere,
and when my mother brings me
some tea my grandmother
will stand in the doorway and ask
if I am hungry, do I want something to eat,
while there in the living room,
where the TV is forever on,
in the light cast by a reading lamp
my grandfather makes
his way through a newspaper
without a date on it.

David Feela

NEAR BEAR'S EARS

I should go there, to the mountain
where the trail to the Bear's Ears begins.
According to friends, it's always busy,
a half-dozen cars or so parked at the trailhead.
The hikers would be climbing the bear's spine
by the time I'd arrive.
I'm a late starter.
I'd be wandering around its ass
glancing up, thinking how much like lice
we hikers must be to the bear
that belongs to those ears.
Once coming up a trail
on the way to Kennebec Pass
a black bear stepped out of the trees
and turned toward me.
I couldn't help it.
My eyes grew wide as caverns.
That bear still lives
inside me,
its breath shallow but steady,
its ears alert,
its eyes turned inward
toward its long cold season
of dreams.

THE OTHER ONE

My left hand looks older,
first time I've noticed this century.
Naturally, I knew it would age,

those fingers opening and closing
like a chorus line, providing
a lifetime of stimulation.
So what did I expect?
Helping out, holding on
while the right one labors for both.

I'm surprised how the veins
have thickened, how the skin
puckers like tissue paper.

Clenched or unclenched,
it does mostly what it's told.
There, it reached

to touch my face.
See how it makes amends?
I forgive you, I forgive you.

Go wrestle with your brother
while I try to figure out
where you left the aspirin.

BEFORE BED

I reach for a toothpick.
During my probe for bits of food
I also uncover lost ideas between my teeth,
fragments from mornings and afternoons.

I don't know why I'm telling you this.
Maybe one evening while poking around
I'll find something tender
that doesn't bleed.

Renee Podunovich

DOWN RIVER
at the Lower Dolores

On the silver feathered backbone
       of an exhale —
            watch grief fly
free as swallows skimming winter waters,
soaring on gales of transience.
Your sorrows released evaporate,
vanish into slickrock, into the mouth
of this river-carved canyon.
        Never ask for them back.

Gather soul medicines found along the path:
rose hips, sage, cedar and lichen
sodden from last night's snow,
their colors momentarily radiant
under melting crystals of frost.
        — Inhale
the vanilla scent of pinion pitch,
a resin that seals the heart,
covers the fissures, restores your tenderness.

Only a scar remains, only noticeable when stars fall,
trails of light across the midnight psyche,
a remnant ache you will keep —
        your own darkness harnessed.
You have learned to wander that precarious edge,
where the conscious and Unconscious meet;
using your subtle body, a place deeper than logic,
and out of obscurity you have scavenged
        a more durable self,
extracted from galaxies and mystery
with the sharp tip of a crescent moon.

Each new year (or day or minute) is an opening,
an opportunity to be bright like river ripples,

sunlit and willingly carried,
held and pushed forward at the same time.
In every moment all facets are happening.
      — Be vast enough —
stretch to contain a dash more shimmer and night.
There is time yet for more,
a day or many; it is unclear
      but we are alive still in air, in water, the fire body,
      in each grateful breath.

ICICLE MEDICINE

I.
She is first a fine snow—
the space between the snowflakes,
the cosmos between the notes in *Für Alina,*
the emptiness inside the complexity of fractals.

Call her cold love to you, let her chill
slide its hands along your spine,
she hunts your warmth, to melt her,
      return her to a river she once was.

Rippling free with summer rain,
soft and dancerly she flowed,
and you remind her of what she will be again
in spring: rapid, lush and reckless.

II.
Everywhere you go,
she is in your cells,
she is your mistress:
the one you sing praises to at dawn,

the one you enter at night,
naked and submissive to her faithful movements,
letting moonbeams and dragonflies
swim with your soul whisperings.

Put your ear to her icy current
and she tells you what is true,
      about your own confused heart.

III.
She takes illusions and freezes them,
each flake a frozen fantasy, a particular
pattern reflecting your wholeness

—what is healed

and the lingering wounds—

the love and the shadows,
they fall around you this early morning in January,
      after the moon was cloaked
      and it was just your unwinding
      and the spiraling stars all night.
This is your gift—
to be holographic,
to hover in the interstitial knowing,
the whole purpose of an icicle
      is to clarify what is fixed,
      shimmering your frozen dream.

Kim O'Connor

FOUR ELEMENTS
       March 23, 2020

I am thinking about Tupperware.
I am thinking about fire and air, earth and water.

Dear fire, when you take everything,
do you take everything? The black field
of your wake is dotted with seeds
we can't see. Right?

It was so windy metal chairs scooted across the deck like clumsy
       oversized crabs.
When the fire or whatever takes everything,
it still leaves the dirty dishes. They still have to be loaded
and unloaded. The Tupperware won't dry
unless it's set out on the dish rack, in the air.

Dogs seem particularly of the earth,
especially this one, who my neighbors found
running with a pack beside a gas station in rural New Mexico;
who came when they called, malnourished, mangy, wagging;
who they dropped off at a shelter while they backpacked for three
       nights;
who they picked up on the way home after no one had claimed him;
who they offered to us to keep because I'd said we could get a dog
"when one came into our lives."

Our house doesn't even really touch the ground: built on the side of
       a hill,
it rests on huge metal stilts. It shakes when
the wind blows hard, which happens often.

Snow is a form of water, my least favorite form,
except for ice, which is worse. When it snows
we are truly stuck inside.

The dog was good at first, and gentle
with the cats. He sniffed the frosty dead
grass stalks for rabbits.

I keep organizing the Tupperware and
it keeps getting messed up, as though
a tiny hurricane blows through the drawer
each night while we sleep.

Dear fire, you can't live without air,
but water is your enemy.

The snow silences the street as the dog and I
walk through it. He would prefer not to be on a leash;
I would prefer not to be outside at all, though
I try to notice how pretty the world is
covered in white, how huge the moon
when the clouds reveal it.

We walk the dog on the mesa.
One foot in front of the other,
we climb up almost every day.

Dear fire, when you take everything,
everything does eventually return,
bringing to mind a tree in winter,
a tree in summer, a tree in spring,
a tree in fall. Is it the same tree,
or a different tree?
It is not a different tree; it is not the same.

When we climb the mesa in the wind advisory,
dirt blows into our eyes and mouths.
We illegally unleash the dog.
We can see the city from up there, shrouded
in light from the sunset, burning.
The dog prances in the troubled air.

Kathleen Cain

A TARBERT EVENING (1986)
for Mary and Tom O'Connell

We'd go in at what seemed late,
seven or seven-thirty, the table set
to perfection. The meal of salmon
("twice-poached" as James Murphy
liked often to joke). The talk limited,
to accommodate the need to eat while
the spuds and veg were still warm, in
the air that washed up from the river.
Was there wind that came and went
with the tides (I wonder now but didn't
then)? There's always a chill near water.

I remember Mary's eyes, the glisten of
her smile as she presided over the feast.
Ban a tí: Woman of the House, in the old
meaning of the word: not landlady, but
true mistress of hearth and table. And Tom,
proud beside her, bringing everything
to hand in ways that showed the rhythm
of the years that flowed between them. Irish
coffee to end the meal, a toast to strangers:
"Ye are the same as we are."

And then the fun began. The others arrived
to start the party. "God bless all here,"
the old people called, as they crowded in the door,
shaking the cold off them, clasping each other
in the goodwill that warmed their spaces
and kept the village whole (though of course
there were whispers—there would always
be whispers). Just who had the first song
I don't recall—the move was seamless
from chat to music. Not announced. Just done.
Each one his or her party piece, and who

couldn't sing might tell a joke or story.
Michael Fitz was best at this. I heard him
go four nights once without repeating
a single hilarity. And who would sing but
couldn't was always helped along, chorus
ever at the ready. And who could sing
but often held back, like James Murphy,
was nearly begged for "Raglan Road,"
and when he would begin pin-drop silence
was his honor, the clear lament in no uncertain
terms, in that unhesitating voice; whose
blind eyes knew darkness like no other.

It would go on that way till sometimes
two or three, when everyone would toddle
home. Back down the village, each and all,
to a nest in the winter night, with the tide,
singing always, its way from shore to shore.

LACE
for RBG

The patterns always grace
a dull demeanor
even lift
a black robe
into other circumstance;
set the wearer apart
so you know exactly
who she is.

Not a doily
but a supreme intricacy
knit from fervor
of mind and hunger
for justice, inspired.

DEAR STRANGER,

Yes, I know your middle name and your address—but only from the public records, so don't be alarmed. I live two states away—or three, depending on the route. I also know you're unlikely to vote. That's why I'm writing. To let you know how you can vote, and when, and all that. The directions said write a few sentences in my own words—without taking sides—about why we vote. That middle part's hard for me, but I'll follow the rules. My reasons are simple. I haven't missed a vote in more than fifty years, and I'm not about to miss one now. I'm not a flag-waver, chest-thumper, anything like that . . . but I do believe that voting is one of the most important things I can do as an American. And it's something we can all do together—a thing that gets harder and harder these days.

I'd like to say more. Much more. About how sorry I am that things are so hard for you there in Texas. Drought. Fires. The aftermath of those two hurricanes (so far) in all those places I heard my mother talk about growing up. Port Arthur (how I loved the way she spoke those two words, in what was left of her drawl—something like "Pourt Ah-thur"—she was a Gainesville girl). Corpus. Houston. And then, I heard on the news how tough it is to vote down there—one drop box per county. I've seen the long lines on TV. How brave you all are, to come out and stand in that heat, or that dust, or that rain, and vote.

Thinking of y'all, that's for sure . . .
Sincerely,
Kathleen C.

Victor Pearn

prayer against corona

maker of wind
that floats clouds
many do not believe what cannot
be seen would hurt or help them

help us to see what you see in others
I am here at the beginning
with you before
the creation of the world

help us to have your mind
to give everyone a place
in the circle with your children
bless those who are dead
bless those who are ill
bless those who are healthy

give us your mind for healing
oh god pour your peace into them
like a soft rain remembered
so that we may see your creation
so that we may touch your presence

DANCING IN THE STREETS

Leaves were
dancing in the streets
tumbleweeds were
flying across the interstate.

At the intersection
of I-25 and highway 34
a man stood holding a
cardboard sign saying,
"I need a miracle."

I had to laugh
thinking
we all do.

I am praying for him
to receive the miracle he needs.

INTEGRITY

Integrity guides us as individuals
and as a nation. When a leader
is a vile person it can cause
others to become distracted from
their own personal integrity
ever so slightly, but just enough to
cause that person not to do their best.
When a leader lacks honesty
it can cause a relaxation in
the honesty of those who follow.
If a nation lacks integrity that nation
will fall. And oh, how far down
can we go? If it is true—ruthless
men gain only wealth—then what?
Every day we need to do our best,
and uphold integrity!

WHO'S IN HEAVEN?

"One two three four five six seven,
all good children go to heaven."
—The Beatles

John and George are practicing
magnificent guitar music,
and John is playing piano.

And they're writing new lyrics.

In perfect timing, waiting
for that moment to arrive when

they'll be reunited
with Paul and Ringo,
forever in Elysium clouds.

Imagine the concerts we'll hear.

Linda Keller

SOMETIMES

Sometimes the light
pushes its arm
through the tree
and the grassy patch
in its hand
begins to glow

Sometimes we want to put
a worn leather saddle on a star
We want to sleep outside
listening to crickets
put the tears in a jar in the cupboard
with the sticky door

We try to remember life
before the curtain of death fell
on its stage

We remember galloping
in the classroom
typing up poems
displaying them on colored paper,
voices our students were finding

Now, I look for my own voice.

I look for the light
dangling between the branches,
the jeweled patches of green
that I know are there.

SACRED SPACE

Clouds drift like ships at sea
above the mountains.
I mark their movement,
how they line up with the peak,
then float down the ridge line.

Footprints of rabbits
and deer in the snow
lift my mouth into a smile.

Wind sings its song
percussion
intensifying
diminishing
the sun, in and out,
like an accent note.
Everything moving
snow melting
tracks disappearing
nothing the same
except the peace
I feel when I'm here.

WHATEVER IT WAS

Maybe it was standing all day
on a floor so hard not even
a plush scrap of carpet could
cushion my feet
Maybe it was the rickety podium
with the feet that wouldn't lock
in place
or the marker board that never
fully washed clean
or that the room had no windows
Maybe it was a combination
of saying and writing instructions
that didn't sink in,
but whatever it was,
I had started to feel half-buried,
like the victim of a summer beach prank
that had gone too far,
a thunderstorm blowing in,
the waves looming closer,
my legs cemented in
the heavy sand,
but this time,
I could feel the motion,
I could see the sand cracking
and it wouldn't be long
before my feet would emerge
and I would take off
running
trying to steal back time
the way a baseball player
tries to slide past one more base
when no one is looking.
Whatever it was,
this time,
the score was for me.

HEADLINES

How newsworthy would this headline be:

9 Trees in Washington Park to Be Cut Down for New Basketball Court

6 are pines: Pinyon and Austrian.

Would it include the fact that these old, old trees
have branches that brush the ground,
that you can stand under them,
like you are inside a living house,
unseen by those who pass by,
that it is a place savored
by those who have not forgotten how to be children —

How can this compete with shutdowns, walls and strikes?

Now this: the shoulders of the backcountry on Vail Pass
held the weight of 32,000,
double from the year before.

Would it be worth noting that on one snowy mile of 6,
I followed the tracks of a bobcat?
That when I saw the way the branches held the snow,
and how the trunks cast blue shadows,
that, in their silence,
they spoke, like a headline.

CONTRIBUTORS

Jean Bell's poetry books include *At Home on Blue Creek*; *Grandma Poems*; *Rainbow Sky: Birding in Southern Costa Rica*; and *Walking into the Wind*. Her most recent book, *Howling at 8 pm*, contains her poems ripped from the headlines in 2020 —pandemic, Black Lives Matter, gender equity, climate change, democracy in danger.

Maria Berardi's work has appeared in local and national magazines, as well as at the Arvada Center for the Arts and Humanities, in Arvada, CO, in collaboration with installation artist Bonnie Ferrill Roman. Her first collection, *Cassandra Gifts*, was published in 2013 by Turkey Buzzard Press; she is at work on her second.

Kathleen Cain stayed sane during the Covid Year by writing daily haiku, sharing National Poetry Month with a group of Nebraska poets and by sitting around the Zoom campfire with The Freewritin' Fools. Her poems have appeared most recently in *Earth's Daughters* and *The Comstock Review*. An anthology with the Nebraska poets is due out shortly.

Frank Coons, poet and veterinarian, is the author of three books of poetry. *Finding Cassiopeia (*2014), published by Lithic Press, was a finalist for the Colorado Book Awards. His second book, *Counting in Dog Years* (2016), published by Lithic Press. The third, *A Flash of Yellow Wing* is in publication from Orchard Street Press. His work has appeared in Caesura, Evening Street Press, Plainsongs, Pensive Journal, Santa Fe Literary Review, Pacific Review, and elsewhere. He was nominated for a Pushcart prize in 2019.

Robert Cooperman's latest collection is *Reefer Madness* (Kelsay Books), part memoir of his misspent youth, part a tale around the fact that the Girl Scouts of Colorado okayed the selling of their cookies outside pot shops. Forthcoming from Apprentice House is *Go Play Outside*, a love letter to Cooperman's lifelong unrequited passion for basketball.

Mike Coste lives in Littleton, Colorado. His works have been published in The Burningword Literary Journal, 34th Parallel, Right Hand Pointing, Drunk Monkeys, Jitter Press, and Dual Coast Magazine. He has also had two short plays produced locally.

Art Elser's poetry has appeared in many journals and anthologies. His books include: *A Death at Tollgate Creek, As the Crow Flies, To See a World in a Grain of Sand, It Seemed Innocent Enough, A High Plains Year in Haiku,* and *It Begins in Silence, Ends in Grace*.

David Feela has published three poetry books, *Thought Experiments,* The Maverick Press, 1998, *The Home Atlas,* WordTech Editions, 2009, and *Little Acres,*

Unsolicited Press, 2018. An essay collection, *How Delicate These Arches,* Raven's Eye Press, 2011 was a finalist for the Colorado Book Award.

Carol Guerrero-Murphy has a significant history of publishing while teaching creative writing from preschool through graduate levels. Her first book, *Table Walking at Nighthawk*, Ghost Road Press, 2007 was nominated for a Pushcart and earned a Willa Award. *Chained Dog Dreams* is her second full length book.

Michael Henry is co-founder and Executive Director of Lighthouse Writers Workshop and the author of two books of poetry: *Active Gods,* and *No Stranger Than My Own,* as well as a chapbook, *Intersection.*

Judyth Hill, poet, editor, teacher, author of acclaimed poem "Wage Peace," and nine books of poetry including: *Tzimtzum,* Mercury Heartlink; *Dazzling Wobble*, Future Cycle Press. She lives in Evergreen, Colorado. President of PEN San Miguel, Hill leads global poetry and Wild Writing retreats. St. Helena Examiner described her as, "Energy with skin," the Denver Post as, "A tigress with a pen."

Linda Hogan, an internationally recognized author and speaker, was a finalist for the Pulitzer Prize with her novel *Mean Spirit.* Her poetry collection *The Book of Medicines* was a National Book Critics Circle Award finalist. Her most recent book of poetry is *A History of Kindness* and before it: *Dark Sweet: New and Selected Poems.* Her novels include: *People of the Whale, Solar Storms,* and *Power.* Essay collections include: *Dwellings: A Spirit History of the Living World* and *The Radiant Lives of Animals.* She has received Guggenheim, Lannan, National Endowment for the Arts, and Native Arts and Culture Fellowships, a PEN Thoreau Award and numerous other recognitions.

Joe Hutchison, Colorado Poet Laureate (2014-2019), has authored 19 poetry collections, including: *The World As Is: New & Selected Poems, 1972-2015; Eyes of the Cuervo/Ojos del Crow* (bilingual edition); and *Marked Men,* poems around the Sand Creek massacre. His new book, *Under Sleep's New Moon,* is forthcoming in 2021. https://www.jhwriter.com

Amy Wray Irish grew up near Chicago, received her MFA from the University of Notre Dame, then fled the Midwest for Colorado sunshine. She has been published recently in Progenitor, Thought for Food, and TwentyBellows Lit. Her third chapbook, *Breathing Fire,* is now available from MiddleCreek Publishing. For more information go to amywrayirish.com.

Anita Jepson-Gilbert, has taught English, from ESL to college writing. She published a bilingual children's book, entitled *Maria and the Stars of Nazca,* which won 1st Place in Children's Books from the Colorado Independent Publishers. She has two chapbooks of poetry: *Places and Faces,* and *Everywoman.* She has been active in creating a statewide poetry community for over 25 years.

Marcia Jones began to write poetry a few years ago. Her poems have won national, state, and local awards and are published in anthologies. In 2020, she published *only time,* a first poetry collection, fall of 2021, she will publish her second book, *Blue Hour,* a collection of poems about her journey with cancer.

Jim Keller has been involved with the Evergreen poetry scene for a couple decades and lately as co-host with Murray Moulding of its Mad Blood poetry venue extension. His book *Camus' Camel* is available on Amazon and at Hearthfire Books in Evergreen.

Linda Keller is the author of 7 books of poetry including: *Mother, Take It and Go On, Comet Dreams,* and *Deep in the Wilderness.* Her poem, "Sometimes" was included in the PITTOC Volume Two international anthology edited by G. A. Cuddy. Linda lives in Denver and tutors students in writing. Her website is ljkeller.com

Peggy Knoepfle's, books include: *Sparks from your Hoofs,* chapbook published by Sangamon Poets; *The Bridge of Isfahan,* by Nilla Cram Cook, and *After Alinsky: Community Organizing in Illinois,* were edited by Peggy Knoepfle; Published by "Illinois Issues Magazine," UIS, Springfield; (A young community organizer named Barack Obama wrote one of the articles in this, highly sought after, extremely rare book). She edited "Illinois Issues Magazine for 17 years, was co-founder of Brainchild a women's poetry collective, and she was a well-known activist in Springfield. Two days after being in an accident riding with a friend, Peggy passed away May 23, 2021, shocking many friends and family members.

Page Lambert, has been writing about the western landscape and leading nature retreats in the west for over 20 years. Her writing can be found online at Huffington Post and inside the pages of dozens of anthologies. Lambert blogs, "All Things Literary/All Things Natural" from her mountain home west of Denver.

Lynda La Rocca, a freelance writer and editor, her poetry has appeared in numerous poetry-society anthologies. Her poetry chapbooks include *The Stillness Between,* 2009, Pudding House Publications, Ohio and *Spiral,* 2012, Liquid Light Press, Colorado. "One Sided-Conversation with COVID-19 (with apologies to Dr. Seuss)" was reprinted in the anthology *Stories from the Age of Covid*; "The Journey" was first published in *A Book of the Year 2013,* by Poetry Society of Texas. La Rocca performs with the poetry troupe River City Nomads and lives in Salida, Colorado.

Kyle Laws directs Line/Circle: Women Poets in Performance. Her collections include: *Ride the Pink Horse,* Stubborn Mule Press, 2019, *Faces of Fishing Creek,* Middle Creek Publishing, 2018, *This Town: Poems of Correspondence,* coauthored with Jared Smith, Liquid Light Press, 2017, *So Bright to Blind,* Five Oaks Press, 2015, *Wildwood,* Lummox Press, 2014 and *Apocalypse of the Snare Drum* 2020, A joint project of Steel City Art Works artists.

John Macker's latest book is *Desert Threnody*, fiction, essays and one-act play. He's author of *Atlas of Wolves*, poems and *The Blues Drink Your Dreams Away, Selected Poems 1983-2018*, finalist for an Arizona/New Mexico Book Award.

Sandra S. McRae writes about nature and domestic complexities, the political and the divine, food, and hunger of all kinds. Her books include *all the way to just about there*, FutureCycle Press, *The Magic Rectangle*, Folded Word, and *Weber's Big Book of Grilling*, Chronicle. She teaches at Red Rocks Community College.

Murray Moulding is a graduate of Cornell and the Iowa Writers' Workshop. He has taught creative writing at colleges in Illinois, Montana, Oregon and Colorado. He lives in Denver and Florida, with his wife, Kate, and their dog, Shakira.

Gia Nold holds a Master of Fine Arts from Naropa University and teaches Visual Arts in Denver Public Schools. She is the author of three chapbooks of poetry including, *Moon is Always Moon*, Green Fuse Poetic Arts.

Kim O'Connor is a North Carolinian who lives in Golden, Colorado. She works for Lighthouse Writers Workshop. Her first book, *White Lung*, is forthcoming from Saturnalia Books in fall 2021.

Veronica Patterson's poetry collections include: *How to Make a Terrarium*, Cleveland State University, *Swan, What Shores?* NYU Press Prize, *Thresh & Hold*, Gell Poetry Prize, *& it had rained*, CW Books, *Sudden White Fan*, Cherry Grove, and two chapbooks. She teaches creative writing for the Osher Lifelong Learning Institute, and is Loveland's first Poet Laureate.

Victor Pearn, has worked as a marine ground-radio repairman, earned the BA in In. O. (the un-program) at Sangamon State University, Springfield, Illinois. Attended summer writer's conference for poets in Boulder, Colorado—fell in love with mountains 40 years. This June with Spirit, one of his four daughters, he walked Mount Margaret 8.8 miles; in July he walked Lawn Lake 13.6 miles.

Renee Podunovich has three chapbooks of poems: *Illustrious for Brief Moments*, Finishing Line Press, 2020, *Let the Scaffolding Collapse*, Finalist of the New Women's Voices Chapbook Competition by Finishing Line Press, 2012, and *If There Is a Center No One Knows Where It Begins*, Art Juice Press, 2008. She is the 2019 Cantor Award winner for the best poem by a Coloradoan in —the Fischer Prize of the Telluride Literary Festival.

Gerard Smaldone, Denver poet, writes about the Mysteries, his family and the city. He has self-published many chapbooks and two screen plays. When he's not advising top-tier thinkers on how to survive the coming global holocaust/ascension physically, spiritually, and financially into the 5th dimension—Gerardo gets beat up by numerous grandchildren.

Jared Smith's 16th volume of poetry will be released this fall by New York Quarterly Books. His work has appeared in hundreds of domestic and inter- national journals and anthologies over the past 25 years. He was selected Judge of the NFSPS Founders Award (2020) and Stevens Manuscript Award (2021.)

Padma Thornlyre, Mad Blood's founder, is the author of several collections of poetry, most recently *The Anxiety Quartet*. A proud member of the literary out- laws known as Fire Gigglers, he co-founded Turkey Buzzard Press and is now living in Raton, New Mexico, finishing his novel, *Baubo's Beach: an autobio- graphy of the unconscious,* and beginning a new collection of poems, *Wagjaw.* He is raising his original *Mad Blood* magazine, published 2003-2006, from the ashes, and expects to debut its reincarnation in 2021.

Bill Tremblay directed the MFA in Creative Writing Program at Colorado State University, founded the *Colorado Review* and served as its chief editor for 15 years. He received the John F. Stern Distinguished Professor Award in 2004. He is the author of a novel, *The June Rise*. His work has appeared in nine full-length volumes including: *Crying in the Cheap Seats, The Anarchist Heart, Home Front, Second Sun: New & Selected Poems, Duhamel: Ideas of Order in Little Canada, Rainstorm Over the Alphabet, Shooting Script: Door of Fire,* which won the Colorado Book Award. He has received fellowships and awards from the NEA, the NEH, the Fulbright Commission, and the Corporation at Yaddo. His work has been featured in many anthologies.

Lon Wartman's favorite pastimes are photography and poetry, in both capturing the moment. He grew up in southwest Kansas in ranching and farming, worked as a commercial appraiser and is now pursuing his lifelong passion of being a photographer/poet and working on his 2nd book of poetry.

Kathryn Winograd, poet and essayist, is the author of six books. Her seventh book, *Flying Beneath the Dog Star*, will be published January 2022 as part of the 2020/2021 Finishing Line Press Open Chapbook Contest.

Lorrie Wolfe is an editor, technical writer and poet. She served as poetry editor for *RISE: An Anthology of Change,* which won *the 2019 Colorado Book Award.* Her chapbook, *Holding: From Shtetl to Santa,* is available at Lorriewolfe.com.

Jon Kelly Yenser lives in Albuquerque. His first collection, The *News As Usual*, was given the Nelson Poetry Award by the Kansas Authors Club. A second book, *Walking Uphill at Noon,* is forthcoming from University of New Mexico Press.

Lisa Zimmerman's poetry and fiction have appeared in many journals and anthologies including *Florida Review, Poet Lore,* and *Cave Wall.* Recent collections include: *The Light at the Edge of Everything,* Anhinga Press, *The Hours I Keep,* and *Sainted,* Main Street Rag 2021. She's a professor at the University of Northern Colorado.